IAIN HYSLOP was born in Glasgow a ...in
apprenticeship in the Clyde Shipyai ...id
safety. He is a graduate of the Open A
lifelong football fan, he has followed the national team at .... id.
He is currently revisiting the Third Division grounds as he follows his club,
Rangers, on their journey back through Scottish football.

The story continues...

Is the Baw Burst?

Volume Two: Rangers Special

A Long-Suffering Supporter Continues the Search

for the Soul of Scottish Football

IAIN HYSLOP

Luath Press Limited

EDINBURGH

www.luath.co.uk

First published 2012

ISBN: 978-1-908373-55-7

The paper used in this book is recyclable. It is made from low chlorine pulps
produced in a low energy, low emissions manner from renewable forests.

The author's right to be identified as author of this book under the Copyright,
Designs and Patents Act 1988 has been asserted.

Printed in the UK by Bell & Bain Ltd., Glasgow

Typeset in 11 point Sabon

To my wife, mum (we all still miss you very much), family, friends and colleagues

Contents

Acknowledgements

A big thank you to everyone at Luath Press for all their help and guidance. Special thanks to Kirsten Graham for diligently compiling and making sense of the mass of documents, photos, spreadsheets and everything else that goes into a volume of *Is The Baw Burst?*

Thanks to all the contributors, especially those who cajoled friends and colleagues to complete the questionnaires and to those who assisted in my never-ending quest for match tickets. In no particular order: Papa Club, Colin McDowall, Alan Pattullo, David Edgar, Andrew Gordon, Graeme McLean, Jim McMahon, Frank Meade, Keith MacDonald, David Cook, David Fox, Scot van den Akker, Alan Davies, Roddy O'Hara, Craig Maclean, David Gow, Richard Cook, Robert McDougall, Paul Martin, Neil Fox, Roy Callaghan, Joe Richardson, Andrew Guy, Alasdair Mitchell, Callum McDougall, Kenny McKie, James Robinson, Colin McCabe, George Wilson, Neil Thomson, Scott Christie, Alexander Bird, David Todd, Terry O'Byrne, Kelly Jones, Stuart Balharrie, Brian Hume, Greg Riddle, Alan Wilson, Alison Fletcher, Jackie Wales and the Big Man.

And to my wife Debbi for putting up with all of this – again! We did enjoy some great 'football' weekends in the caravan though, highly recommended.

2012 Timeline

13 February   It is reported that Rangers are considering going into administration after papers are lodged at the Court of Session in Edinburgh.

14 February   Administrators Duff and Phelps are appointed after a court battle with Her Majesty's Revenue and Customs. The SPL immediately deduct ten points from Rangers, leaving them 14 behind Celtic.

8 March   The SFA declare Rangers owner Craig Whyte unfit to hold a position at a football club and confirm that the club is facing a charge of bringing the game into disrepute.

9 March   Duff and Phelps announce a package of players' wage cuts that prevent substantial job losses at Rangers Football Club.

15 March   The SFA issue Rangers with notices of complaint over alleged breaches of disciplinary rules.

4 April   Rangers administrators confirm they have received four bids for the football club.

23 April   Rangers are handed a transfer embargo for 12-months (on signing players).

13 May   The administrators announce that a binding contract selling the club to his consortium has been signed by former Sheffield United chief executive Charles Green.

16 May   Rangers' appeal against a £160,000 fine and 12-month transfer embargo is rejected by the SFA.

29 May   The Court of Session SFA rules the transfer ban unlawful following a challenge from Rangers. Duff and Phelps publish Charles Green's Company Voluntary Arrangement (CVA) proposal.

30 May   The SPL clubs choose to take on responsibility for deciding whether 'newco' clubs should be admitted to the competition. Fixed penalties are rejected.

12 June   HMRC announce that the CVA offer will be rejected and the club face liquidation.

14 June   The consortium led by Charles Green completes the takeover of Rangers' assets and business following the club's liquidation.

15 June	Ally McCoist commits his future to the club.
18 June	The SPL confirm a vote will take place on 4 July on whether to admit newco Rangers to the league. A provisional fixture list will be released with 'Club 12' replacing Rangers.
22 June	Hearts and Dundee United indicate their intention to veto Rangers' application to play in the SPL.
24 June	Rangers players Steven Whittaker and Steven Naismith reject a transfer to the newco, claiming they are now free agents. Hibernian confirm they will oppose the newco Rangers application to the SPL.
25 June	The Crown Office instruct Strathclyde Police to conduct a criminal investigation into Craig Whyte's takeover of Rangers and the subsequent financial management of the club. Inverness and Aberdeen indicate that they will oppose Charles Green's SPL application. Newco Rangers will start life outside the top flight.
4 July	It is reported that the SPL clubs vote 'overwhelmingly' to reject the newco Rangers application to the league after lengthy talks at Hampden.
17 July	Rangers discuss membership of Division Three with the SFA and SFL.
21 July	Rangers' hopes of SFA membership hang in the balance.
26 July	Brechin City manager Jim Weir and assistant manager Kevin McGowne are keen for Sunday's proposed Ramsdens Cup tie with Rangers to go ahead.
27 July	Rangers granted conditional SFA membership, which will allow Sunday's televised Cup tie with Brechin City to go ahead.
29 July	Brechin City host Rangers in the first round of the Ramsdens Cup.
7 August	Rangers welcome East Fife to Ibrox for their first home game of the season in the League Cup.
11 August	Division Three kicks off for Rangers at Balmoor Stadium in Peterhead.
8 November	Red Flag Alert Football Distress Survey finds that six Scottish football clubs are showing signs of financial uncertainty.
20 November	Old Rangers win their appeal against the tax bill presented to them for the use of Employee Benefit Trusts.

Introduction

Welcome to Volume 2 of *Is the Baw Burst?* – the unofficial review of Scottish football. The original journey in season 2010/11 captured many aspects that needed to be addressed for the good of the game. Change was required. The murmurings were getting louder. Fans were fed up with our national sport – it was stale. But what should be done? No one could agree. Things just trundled along as usual; early knockouts from European competitions, hopeless qualification campaigns for international tournaments and the Old Firm dominating the major prizes.

Season 2011/12 started like every other one for the past few years. The league flag was unfurled at Ibrox by a rather startled looking chap called Craig Whyte. He would go on to make a significant contribution to events. Whyte had recently purchased Rangers for the princely sum of £1 from the weary Sir David Murray. Players were signed, new contracts issued and generally, things were looking rosy in the garden of Ibrox for the Scottish champions.

There was one small thing though. Her Majesty's Revenue and Customs were very interested in some of the financial dealings of the club over the past decade. This annoying little thorn kept pricking away at the side of the world famous institution. Then, in February 2012, the Glasgow giants imploded in spectacular fashion. Rangers Football Club went into administration. Scottish football was rocked to the core. Our national game would never be the same again. Has the baw finally burst?

Timeline

It was early February and rumours were rife about financial wrongdoings past and present at Ibrox. The team had also thrown away a massive lead over Celtic in the league – something wasn't right. In a few short months Rangers' promising new beginning under the stewardship of Craig Whyte had disintegrated. Nikica Jelavic had just departed for Everton in a multi-million pound deal. In October 2011, the big

Croatian had famously said that the league was over when Rangers were 15 points clear of their city rivals, Celtic. In hindsight, his confidence was understandable. Celtic were struggling and their manager, Neil Lennon, was minutes away from throwing in the towel during a match at Rugby Park in which they trailed Kilmarnock 3-0. A remarkable turnaround that day meant the game ended in a 3-3 draw. Celtic never looked back. Rangers have been going backwards ever since.

On 14 February, I got two text messages in quick succession. Both read exactly the same: 'Rangers in admin'. I was running a course so had little time to digest the news until later in the day. Despite the many rumours that this would be the outcome, it was still hard to swallow. Craig Whyte had lodged papers indicating that he was thinking about administration the day before. I had honestly expected an 11th-hour intervention from a 'blue-nosed' consortium or a Russian oligarch. It wasn't to be. That St Valentines Day heralded the start of months and months of despair for so many people directly and indirectly associated with the club. Sir David Murray, what were you thinking about?

One of the first respondents to the crisis was Murray himself. He expressed surprise and disappointment at the club's predicament and admitted making a 'huge mistake' in selling Rangers to Craig Whyte. The former owner insisted he was 'duped' by the Motherwell-born businessman before he handed over his majority shareholding in the Ibrox club for £1 last May. 'I wish I'd never done the deal with Craig Whyte', said Murray.

He continued, 'my advisers were duped, the bank was duped, the shareholders were duped. Weve all been duped.' Former Rangers director Dave King thought otherwise, saying: 'I do not believe that there will be a single person in Scotland who has dealt with both gentlemen that would believe that Craig Whyte had the capacity to dupe David Murray.'

Manager Ally McCoist was defiant. 'We will be doing everything to make sure Rangers comes out the other side far better and far stronger', he said. His stance galvanised the fans and would prove pivotal in the following tumultuous months. The title dream was over, predicted nine-in-a-row captain Richard Gough. 'Rangers in administration is a tragedy', said Sir Alex Ferguson. SFA chief executive Stewart Regan said 'the Rangers crisis may change rules'. He also predicted 'Armageddon' for the game in Scotland.

Such was the magnitude of the situation that everybody had something to say, none more so than the fans. Ibrox was sold out the following Saturday. Rangers were in administration and the club was on the brink of extinction – 140 years of history could go down the plughole. This great institution was on its knees and Scottish football had, arguably, hit an all-time low. But as usual the fans responded and filled the stadium. 'We don't do walking away' was the quote from manager Ally McCoist, also a former player and fan. And he's right; the fans never walk away. That's always done by people with no real interest in the club beyond self-gain and who are prepared to milk them for every penny. Things got worse over the coming months.

The coverage of events at Rangers was incessant and extremely irritating. Newspaper columns, phone-ins, TV and radio programmes featured little else. Almost daily, there was 'new' interest from parties looking to take over the club. I didn't know who or what to believe. The team's performances on the pitch were also suffering. Many of the players had taken massive wage cuts to keep the club going but the uncertainty was getting to everyone. Football had become a sideshow.

Meanwhile, the reality of the situation began to sink in. A ten point deduction was one of the first penalties administered. A transfer embargo was imposed and the right to participate in European competition was taken away. Duff and Phelps, the administrators, arrived on the scene and the talking continued. Company voluntary agreements (CVAs) were mentioned. Some said liquidation was inevitable. Elsewhere, others were sharpening their claws.

Some of the SPL clubs saw the situation as an opportunity to change the voting structure of the league. Ten of the twelve stated that they 'remain united for change'. This breakaway group, which excluded Celtic, became known as 'the SPL ten'. They pounced on the uncertainty at Rangers and arranged a series of meetings to discuss voting rights. The fallout from the transfer embargo continued. Administrator David Whitehouse argued:

> The decision to prohibit the club from signing new players is akin to a court ordering the administrator of a trading company not to buy stock. The principal operating and trading asset of a football club are its players and an inability to sign new players frustrates both the ability of the company to trade and the statutory objectives of administration.

I was of the opinion that handing out punishments would only further burden the club and reduce the likelihood of it exiting administration in a positive manner. This would eventually prove to be the case.

Kilmarnock chairman Michael Johnston still thought it was likely that Rangers would remain in the top flight, even if it was in the guise of a newly formed company. 'Members see the commercial benefits of having Rangers, even as a newco,' Johnston told BBC Scotland. 'The clubs are mindful of a sporting integrity aspect but the commercial benefits may outweigh that.' The phrase 'sporting integrity' was now appearing in almost all of the headlines, and fans from every club in Scotland were motivated by it.

Rangers manager Ally McCoist accepted there would be opposition from fans of other clubs should the Ibrox side remain in the SPL as a newco. But he contended:

> I totally understand their opinion but the harsh reality is that their clubs might go to the wall if we go to Division Three. That in no way, shape or form should be looked on as me making some sort of threat, far from it. I can totally understand the opinion of the supporters of other clubs saying we should be punished and maybe put down another couple of divisions. But, in many ways, they should be careful what they wish for because would four or five of the clubs in the SPL survive? I'm not so sure.

I wasn't so sure either. Lots of club chairmen were also worried but the fans had made up their minds. They wanted Rangers out no matter the cost.

Neil Lennon hoped Rangers would sort out their problems in order to keep the Old Firm spectacle alive. But the pressure from the rest was building. Dundee United and Hearts had gone public with their views and, along with Aberdeen, had decided to vote against a newco Rangers being admitted to the Scottish Premier League. The Dons told BBC Scotland that maintaining the integrity of the competition was behind their decision! Motherwell said they could face administration if they could not 'replace significant amounts of income' once the status of the Rangers newco was decided. The Well needed Rangers in the SPL. Things were getting very messy.

The story rumbled on into June when HMRC rejected the proposed company voluntary agreement (CVA). This effectively ended the original Rangers and a newco was born. Charles Green was now the man at the helm. The gruff Yorkshireman with the blunderbuss approach quickly set about rebuilding the club. The team would still play at

Ibrox and train at Murray Park, but which league would they play in? On 4 July, SPL chairmen met at Hampden to vote on the new club's application to replace the old Rangers in the top league. Unfortunately for the new Rangers, according to a BBC Scotland report, ten of the twelve SPL clubs were in opposition to them re-joining that league. The SFL beckoned. There was talk of allowing them into Scottish Division One in the coming season. That was short-lived, and few weeks later they were voted into the fourth tier of senior football in Scotland and granted conditional membership of the SFA. Their new season would begin at Brechin in the Ramsdens Cup on Saturday 29 July.

The fall-out continued and I agreed wholeheartedly with Falkirk manager Steven Pressley's comments. 'There's a great opportunity here for change that can move this country forward for years to come,' he said. 'There's been no vision from those at the top and it really disappoints me.' Former SFA president George Peat was saddened and perplexed by the row over where to place a newco Rangers. 'Out of this awful situation Rangers find themselves in, there is a real chance to restructure the game and complete the final part of the McLeish Report.' But it wasn't to be and another opportunity was missed – will we ever learn?

The first game at Ibrox was an emotional one. East Fife were the visitors on the night and they felt the full force of the Rangers revival. Kick-off was delayed 20 minutes to allow the huge crowd to enter. Nearly 40,000 turned up to see the first round of the League Cup on a warm sunny Tuesday evening. Defiance emanated from the four stands. Bob Marley's classic 'Three Little Birds' boomed out over the PA system. Rangers were back and every little thing was gonna be alright.

A trip north to Peterhead raised the curtain on the league season. East Stirlingshire were then welcomed to Ibrox for the first home match in Division Three. Two cup victories against Falkirk (home and away) came either side of a trip to England to face the Wee Rangers in Berwick. Games were coming thick and fast and the fans were loving it. There was a freshness to the proceedings. Next up were Elgin (home) and Annan (away). It was the biggest game in the history of the Dumfriesshire side and they almost shocked the Glasgow giants. A few days later, their neighbours from Dumfries (Queen of the South) caused one of the biggest upsets in Scottish football after a thrilling penalty shoot-out at Ibrox. Rangers tumbled out of the only cup competition that they were favourites to win – things were grim.

But another two home wins followed, against Montrose and Motherwell, and spirits were raised again. The scalp of the SPL side was a major coup – the new Rangers could mix it with the big boys. A narrow victory over the Mechanics in Forres preceded the inevitable away defeat. Stirling Albion were the perpetrators of, arguably, the worst result in the history of the Glasgow club. The rollercoaster ride continued.

Queen's Park returned to Ibrox on league duty for the first time in over 50 years. The original Glasgow derby attracted the biggest crowd of the season so far. The home team emerged victorious and headed to Cumbernauld the following week to face another old city adversary, Clyde. Two goals won it for the visitors but more importantly, the monkey was off their back. They had managed an away victory in the league for the first time this season – it was nearly November!

Then another crushing defeat. Inverness Caledonian Thistle travelled to Ibrox for the quarter-final of the League Cup and ran out easy winners. The form team in the SPL had shattered the fragile confidence of the Third Division leaders. The manager asked us all to adjust our expectation levels. This was duly done as we prepared for the visit of Second Division high-flyers Alloa. A triumvirate of cup defeats was avoided when the Gers smashed seven past the Clackmannanshire side. Onwards and upwards for Rangers but what about the rest?

The Fans

How will Scottish football fare with Rangers in the bottom division? It is an intriguing question and there has been so much talk about it over the past few months that it is difficult to come to any conclusions. I decided it was time to ask the fans. Volume 1 of *Is the Baw Burst?* was my personal journey. Volume 2 is a joint effort and it has been enlightening. As I followed Rangers on their new journey, I gathered the views of fans along the way. These people from many different clubs have contributed with their own thoughts and theories on how best to improve the game in this country. As you would expect, there is a wide-ranging set of viewpoints. Consensus will be difficult but it is achievable because basically everyone wants the same thing – improvements to our national sport.

One of the burning questions relates to an SPL without Rangers. How will some of the less financially stable clubs survive without the two visits from the Glasgow team over the course of a season?

The directors at Motherwell and Kilmarnock have worried about the potential lost revenue. The recent Red Flag Alert Football Distress Survey highlights that the relegation of Rangers has had some impact. Lower attendances and falling revenues and, in particular, the reduction in TV money has given rise to the distress that is spread across the SPL and Divisions One and Two. I'm sure there will be more upheaval for Scottish football in the coming months.

But the fans see it differently. Yes, more of them will need to go and support their clubs to make up for the shortfall caused by Rangers. But almost all are positive about this. They are relishing the chance to finish higher up the league and they have better prospects of landing one of the other major prizes. The Old Firm dominance has changed. Celtic will be much stronger than the rest whereas Rangers are now firmly in amongst the chasing pack. This will be good short term but, as I've said before, the two Glasgow giants are far too big for the game in this country and need to move on. Most fans, including myself, agree that their dominance has been detrimental to the game as whole and want them out of Scottish football.

At the other end of Scottish football, in the Third Division, clubs have been revitalised. A visit from the Glasgow giants guarantees a sell-out crowd and huge interest from all over the country and beyond. So far, it's been great for these smaller clubs and this backs up the argument for extending the size of the leagues. The players raise their game when they're facing Rangers, fans get to visit different places and, arguably more importantly, it has freshened things up by relieving the monotony of the SPL.

The liquidation of Rangers has also raised awareness of the importance of 'living within one's means'. Across the board, fans stated the importance of prudent financial management. They are fully aware of the consequences of mismanagement – 'if it can happen to Rangers, it can happen to anyone'. This is pleasing to know, as sentiment can sometimes get in the way of rational thought when it comes to your team. For too long it has been acceptable to strive for success whatever the cost. This attitude is changing. There is a much stronger focus on the business side of things – artificial pitches are a good example of this. They bring in much needed revenue and become a focal point for their local communities. They encourage a good style of football as well. Again, the fans have picked up on these benefits and would like to see more artificial pitches throughout the country.

Foreign players and the influence they've had (or not had) have for a long time divided the opinions of supporters in this country. Most fans are of the belief that we should concentrate on developing our own young players, as the majority of imports have left a lot to be desired. And whilst there have been some notable exceptions, who have enthralled us with their skills and play, the impact that foreign players have had on the game in Scotland has overwhelmingly been negative. For too long, young Scottish talent has been thwarted because teams have decided to use overseas players. The fans want to see an end to this and the clubs should take note.

Summer football is another topic that divides opinion, but I can now see a shift in favour of changing the time of year when we play football. My preference is March to November and this is not just weather related. Some fans consider that an earlier start would be beneficial for the annual European competitions, as players will have moved beyond the start-of-season lethargy and be playing at their best by the time the qualifiers begin. Others have looked to Scandinavian countries and the improvements that are evident in these regions where football is played outwith the winter months.

Ticket prices remain firmly on the agenda. Fans think football is still too expensive in this country. Prices at Ibrox have fallen significantly due to the club's Third Division status. Early indications are that this has brought more fans through the turnstiles, particularly families, which is great. It's certainly a lot easier on the finances going to see Rangers, both at home and away, this season and long may it continue. But it's a difficult one for the clubs. Will there be enough extra fans attending to make up for the reduced ticket prices, particularly at 'smaller' clubs?

The final point that struck me as I collected the views of the fans, is that leadership, or lack of, continues to dominate their thoughts. Many were disgruntled by the governing bodies' handling of the Rangers situation, particularly the conduct of the SFA and SPL. The SFA have had further bad press due to the events surrounding the recent departure of national coach Craig Levein. Something's got to change and soon. Yet another great opportunity for changes that could have moved football forward in this country has been missed. The crisis at Rangers should have been the catalyst for a fundamental rethink on the future of the game. But, as usual, those at the top lacked leadership and vision and that really disappoints me.

There's More to Life than Fitba

Meanwhile, an excellent European Championship took place in Poland and Ukraine. Euro 2012 provided us with some fabulous games of football, most notably the final when Spain produced a footballing masterclass not seen since the Pelé-inspired Brazil of the 1970s. Indeed many commentators suggested that this was the finest football team ever. And who can argue? Three major championships in a row (two Euros and a World Cup) all won whilst playing an intricate high speed passing game – beautiful. Sadly, the Tartan Army were sitting at home as the drama unfolded in Eastern Europe.

Then the Olympics came along. London welcomed the sporting world and showcased sport at the zenith. Team GB was outstanding and their efforts will hopefully inspire the next generation of sportspeople – tremendous. But back in Scotland, all and sundry were still arguing about Rangers. This once mighty football club was on its knees and many were trying to kick it into the history books for good. Oh and by the way – it was all in the name of sporting integrity!

The events of the past few months at Ibrox have rocked Scottish football to the core. The world famous Glasgow Rangers are now plying their trade in the Third Division. Two years ago, when I embarked on the first stage of my journey to discover if the baw was burst, I commented on the perilous state that the game in Scotland was in. No one in their wildest dreams could have predicted that one of the most successful clubs, ever, would be in such a lowly state. The repercussions will be felt throughout the national game and only time will tell if football in this country will ever fully recover.

So here I go again back to Peterhead, Berwick, Annan and the rest. Places that I visited during the first review but never expected to go back to – certainly not with Rangers! It's been intriguing so far though and the journey will continue until the question is answered – *Is the Baw Burst?*

KILMARNOCK V DUNDEE

Great Expectations

HERE WE GO AGAIN. Scottish Premier League season 2012/13 was about to burst into life. The talking had relented, albeit temporarily, and it was good to be back at a game. But this was no ordinary game. Kilmarnock FC were hosting Dundee FC at Rugby Park and the reality of the fixture meant that Rangers Football Club would be plying their trade in the fourth tier of Scottish football.

Almost two years ago, at Somerset Park on the first day of season 2010/11, I commented on the fact that our national game was in the doldrums. We had to act to make improvements and this has never been more apparent. Never in my wildest dreams could I have predicted the chaos that would unfold over season 2011/12 and prompt me to attend today's game. Dundee Football Club (referred to as Club 12 for the past few weeks) took the place of the once mighty Rangers in the top tier. The liquidated Scottish giants, reformed as a new company, had been refused entry to the Premier Division and would begin a new chapter in their history in Scottish Football League Division Three – oh how the mighty have fallen. Now, more than ever, we must ask the question: *Is The Baw Burst?*

So, Rugby Park it was for the first game of a new review. We'd been on holiday, down the coast in the caravan but I managed to sweet-talk the wife into packing up a wee bit earlier so I could make the 3pm kick-off. Incredibly, the new Rangers had kicked off their season at the bowling green stadium the previous Sunday – Brechin City were the hosts. The newly formed Division Three side pulled off the first 'cup shock' of the season by beating, in extra time, the Division Two outfit in round one of the Ramsdens Cup. Unfortunately, I missed the start of this new era. We were over on Arran at the time so I couldn't make the sell-out game, although I did catch the second half on TV. BBC Alba were showing the game live, but the commentary was in Gaelic and it was all a bit strange – it was shaping up to be one of those seasons!

My last visit to Rugby Park was during a lengthy cold snap in November 2010 so it was nice to be heading back on a beautiful summer's day. En route, I listened to *Off the Ball* and was delighted to hear Ross County chairman Roy McGregor wax lyrical about community based business models being the way forward for football clubs – my sentiments exactly. Volume 1 of *Is The Baw Burst?* highlighted this point and I've since noticed a few clubs talking about this type of arrangement – hopefully the message will get through.

Ten minutes after leaving the house I found myself at a dead end. The wife had given me directions – a shortcut to miss all the traffic! But all was not lost. A few other cars parked beside me and it was then I noticed some Killie fans heading through a gap in the foliage. Excellent. It turned out that there was a small footbridge over a burn and into a housing estate which would take me straight up to the main entrance. Just as I approached the bridge, two coaches turned the corner and screeched to a halt. Straightaway, the contents of the buses spilled out onto the street and headed for the bushes. The Dundee fans had obviously partaken of a few shandies on the journey south and were relieved to get off. Their chanting and clapping immediately raised the decibel levels and, more importantly, heightened the excitement for the home fans. Somehow they managed to keep it up whilst watering the vegetation.

After a leisurely ten minute stroll, I was at the main entrance to the ground. The fans were milling around talking, buying fanzines and programmes and generally just enjoying the good weather. I had expected it to be a bit livelier. The previous season had been a good one for Kilmarnock. A thrilling League Cup final victory over Celtic and seventh place in the league were good foundations to build on. And with Rangers now out of the equation there was no reason why they shouldn't be involved in the scrap for second place. The subdued atmosphere was possibly down to the fact that the club is still heavily in debt and the fans seem to be at odds with the chairman on a number of issues, the main one being his apparent willingness to let newco Rangers into the SPL. Only time will tell if his assessment, based on financial implications rather than sporting integrity, was the correct one.

I purchased the obligatory programme and was heading for the

Club 12 cometh to Kilmarnock.

Moffat Stand when a shout from one of the fanzine vendors caught my attention. 'Whit are you daeing here?' he called to a passing chap. The response was a subdued, 'naewhere else to go.' I can only assume he was a Rangers fan and didn't fancy what was going to be on show at Ibrox over the course of the season. I wondered how many Rangers fans would feel the same way or if it was down to the fact that the SFL season kicked off the following week – again only time will tell.

£17 got me through the turnstile (£3 cheaper than my last visit) and I went straight to the snack bar. After a short wait (spent listening to two Killie fans discussing the Rangers situation) I purchased a Killie Pie and a Bovril, which were the same price as last time (programme was as well), and headed up into the stand. The place was filling up nicely but again it was the Dee fans (nearly 2,000 of them) that were creating the buzz. I was about to take my seat when I noticed that it was covered in bird poo and dust! I quickly selected another one only to find that it also had a thick coating of grime – does nobody clean them once in a while? I moved along a few seats but the situation was the same. No option but to use my pristine white handkerchief – it was great being back at the football!

The game got underway on an immaculate pitch. It was typical start of the season football; slower in almost every sense, misplaced passes, mistimed tackles and very few clear-cut chances. Both teams were trying to play football which was encouraging and the Dundee fans were lively throughout the first half. I thought back to the Kilmarnock teams that I'd seen over the past couple of seasons. There was no way that this lot were anywhere near as good. This constant turnover of players isn't good for the clubs, players or the game itself. All credit to Dundee though. They had put together a team (in a matter of days) that they hoped would go the distance in the SPL.

The half-time whistle was a relief. Things hadn't clicked on the pitch, particularly for the home side who were really labouring. Dundee had had a few breakaways but nothing to get excited about. I turned my attention to the programme as the gloom deepened. The distant sky was black and it looked to be heading in the direction of Rugby Park. I enjoyed reading the programme. There's nothing like the anticipation of a new season to whet the appetite. There was also a strange (figures were out of date) but interesting article on attendances. It focused on how many more supporters Kilmarnock would need to offset the shortfall caused by Rangers' elimination from the top division. A few hundred per match is all they would require – worth watching.

The second half got underway and the stadium crackled into life. Unfortunately it wasn't the football that got the supporters going. The close proximity of the lightning had everyone on the edge of their seats. Torrential rain followed. The storm passed quickly and normal service was resumed. Misplaced passes, mistimed tackles...

Near the end, the goalies had a couple of saves to make and that was the first game over. The final whistle sounded to lots of cheering from the away support. Dundee had a point on the board.

I headed for the car in the rain. The SPL was up and running for the first time without Rangers – strange days indeed.

Quote of the day – *Two Kilmarnock fans: 'I think we should dae a Rangers, liquidate ourselves and start again.' 'Whit?' 'Think aboot it, nae debt, we'd be winning leagues, scoring hunners a goals and we could even stay the night in Arbroath again.' The mind boggles!*

GAME	KILMARNOCK VERSUS DUNDEE
COMPETITION	SPL
DATE	SATURDAY 4 AUGUST 2012, KO 3PM
VENUE	RUGBY PARK
ATTENDANCE	6,523
SCORE	0-0

Some Views from the Fans

Alan Pattullo, age 39, sports writer

CLUB *Dundee.*

SEASON TICKET HOLDER *No.*

FIRST GAME

Liverpool v West Brom, 1981.

FIRST DUNDEE GAME

Dundee v Montrose, August 1983.

BEST MEMORY

Dundee 2 Dundee United 1, Skol Cup quarter-final, 1987. A full-house at Dens, an equaliser for Dundee in the last minutes through Tommy Coyne, and then extra-time winner from Keith Wright.

WORST MEMORY

Probably against the same team, and in the same season. Scottish Cup semi-final at Tynecastle. 2-1 up at half-time, 3-2 down at full-time. Hopes of a first cup since 1973 gone.

BEST FOOTBALL QUOTE

'It's not the losing that hurts, it's the hope that kills us.'

IS THE BAW BURST?

No, this season has proved there are signs of life.

How will the situation at Rangers affect Dundee Football Club?
Quite significantly, as it turns out. Their ejection from the SPL meant Dundee were parachuted in from not just second place in the First Division, but a distant second to the promotion winners Ross County. So far, the fears that Dundee might be ill-prepared – they were handed just a fortnight to make the necessary alterations to the squad – have been played out. Suddenly, the prospect of a season riding high in the First Division has been replaced by the reality of a tough campaign trying to avoid relegation. For many, the initial excitement has been replaced by a sense of dread at the thought of such a long, hard campaign.

How will the situation at Rangers affect Scottish football?
It's certainly not the Armageddon scenario envisaged by the likes of Stewart Regan. Newspapers seem to have had the most trouble coping with the new arrangement and trying to figure out how much coverage should be given to what is now a Third Division club. Crowds seem to have held up in the top league and clearly have been boosted by Rangers' presence in the bottom division

Dundee have been in administration twice in recent years. How does their situation compare to the one at Ibrox?
Dundee, thankfully, were never quite so badly in debt to HMRC, which meant the club had a fighting chance of managing to push through a CVA proposal. The fans seemed to be more active in the Dundee case because it was quite clear that what was needed on each occasion was money. Their fund-raising kept the club afloat. It all seemed – and was – a lot more murky in the Rangers case. It's clear who were the biggest victims in each lamentable episode – the fans, many of the players and those small businesses who had supported both clubs for years.

What do we need to do to improve Scottish football?
It's a pipe dream, and it involves having to try and put the genie back in the bottle, but I sometimes long for a period of time when there are no live games on TV, and everyone has to go to the ground to watch their team at 3pm on a Saturday afternoon. People are so bewildered by shifting kick-off times that they are finding it easy not to go at all. And then stick Sportscene back on a Saturday night...

Colin McDowall, age 49, nurse manager

CLUB   *Kilmarnock FC.*

SEASON TICKET   *Yes.*

FIRST GAME

Partick Thistle v Killie 1969.

BEST MEMORY

May 1997 Scottish Cup Final.

WORST MEMORY

May 2011, Rangers winning the league at Rugby Park. Their fans behaved like animals.

BEST FOOTBALL QUOTE

'You run like you are pulling a caravan.'

IS THE BAW BURST?

Nearly.

How will the situation at Rangers affect Kilmarnock Football Club?
Financially – however this is short term as financially Killie are in trouble regardless of the Rangers situation. Apart from that, not at all.

How will the situation at Rangers affect Scottish football?
Short term financial loss. The TV companies agreeing to show Third Division football will embarrass Scottish football nationally.

You've followed Kilmarnock in the lower leagues – what can Rangers expect?
- Tight playing surfaces.
- Small crowds but passionate local fans.
- Dreadful conditions for fans.
- However, it is worth mentioning I never missed one game when Killie were in the bottom leagues. It was a great experience at the time although I would not like to repeat it.

What do we need to do to improve Scottish football?
- Break the Old Firm monopoly.
- Change the league structure – a top league of 16 would be my choice –

outside of that reduce the number of clubs to form a semi pro league.

- Concentrate funding to the top league – sorry, that may sound elitist but if we are to get back to anything like the glory days funding must improve.
- Reduce prices to attend a match, this might just get more people through the gates.

2

RANGERS V EAST FIFE

Alive, Kicking and Defiant

It was a new dawn at Ibrox and East Fife were the visitors for the first round of the Scottish Communities League Cup. It was also the first home game for the 'new' Rangers. With the SPL getting underway the previous Saturday, Ally McCoist and his players were keen to get going again after the eventful Ramsdens Cup outing at Brechin the weekend before. The fans were also itching to get back to the normality of football after the spring and summer of discontent. 'Rangers will rise again', claimed the new chairman Malcolm Murray and there was genuine excitement in and around the stadium. He also stated that the revival had generated interest amongst supporters worldwide; I'll take his word on that one. The local interest was phenomenal, that was clear to see – I was genuinely taken aback. However, I did wonder about the lack of serious bidders for the club when it was on its knees. Surely more people could see the potential? So all credit to the new regime, they stuck up the money and are custodians of the club. Only time will tell if it's the right move for the Rangers.

Enough about politics, back to the fitba and it was good to see the old place was buzzing. I'd dropped by at lunchtime to collect pre-booked tickets and was amazed by the crowds at the ticket office. Fortunately, I didn't have to wait in the queues (they were still there 20 minutes after the scheduled kick-off time). The service at the pick-up point was swift and I was delighted to collect four tickets for the ludicrously cheap price of £38. Yes, two adults (£12.50 each) and two kids (£6.50 each), I'll say it again – £38. Last season at top SPL games you could pay a similar price for a single ticket, refreshments and pro-gramme. All of a sudden, supporting Rangers had become significantly

The price is right!

cheaper and therefore affordable for more people – it looked like this could be a very interesting season indeed.

I headed back to the stadium after work but arrived way too early. I stayed in the car and listened to one of the football shows on the radio. It quickly became apparent that this was no ordinary game. All and sundry were intrigued by the prospect of a Rangers team, bereft of many of the players that had brought them so much success in recent years, slugging it out in the lower echelons of Scottish football. How would all of this pan out? I decided to hone my thoughts over a beer and headed for an old haunt.

The Swallow Hotel was quiet and I thoroughly enjoyed my pint whilst reminiscing about past glories that had been celebrated in this very bar. League deciders (some decided on goal difference), Champions League matches and pre-season friendlies against the elite of European football were commonplace. Tonight, and the next few seasons, would be very different but there was still much optimism. Sentiment plays a huge part in football and I was sure that this was fuelling the aforementioned confidence.

A text message reminded me of the fact that I had tickets for other people. I left the hotel and headed for John Grieg's statue to meet up with a friend and his two nephews from Germany (I wondered if they knew 'the bouncy'). We headed round to the family section at the Broomloan end and were dismayed to find massive queues. It reminded me of Hampden – what was going on? A cash turnstile was in operation and this was causing the mayhem. The Rangers fans had turned out in their thousands, empathically proving that their club was still alive – game on!

Twenty minutes after the scheduled kick-off time we were still standing. The place was rocking and they had to open up the club deck to let everybody in. What a turnout for a midweek game. One can only assume it was due to the fact that the Fifers were in the league above and an upset was on the cards! The PA system was blaring out classics from the Rangers repertoire. The old favourites were occasionally interrupted by iconic pop songs all featuring a struggle or a fight back.

The music captured the mood very well – defiance – Rangers were back but had they ever really gone away?

The game started at a high tempo that was, no doubt, down to the electric atmosphere. The singing continued unabated and the Rangers players responded with two goals in the opening 45 minutes. It was pretty much one-way traffic towards the East Fife goal for the entire match and Rangers added another two in the second period. All in all, a satisfying result in their first home game of what would be a peculiar season. Four goals, almost 40,000 in the stadium and new quality players on show (many of whom were signed from SPL clubs). East Fife manager Gordon Durie later commented on facing the new Rangers; '[we] are not going to come up against that quality week-in, week-out'. Much food for thought.

So the Third Division side trounced the Second Division side in an enjoyable contest – was the previous week's struggle in Brechin a one-off? Would the East Fife result set the tone for the season? From a Rangers point of view it was very entertaining and that's something that has been sadly lacking over recent seasons. Competing against different teams, scoring goals and playing the game at a high tempo has many positives for the supporters. OK, it might get embarrassing if the score-lines start resembling rugby results but I'm certain that the 'smaller' teams will raise their games, particularly at home, and the matches shouldn't be foregone conclusions. Peterhead on Saturday was already an intriguing prospect.

Quote of the day – *Rangers supporters singing: 'We gonnae win the league'.*

GAME	RANGERS VERSUS EAST FIFE
COMPETITION	SCLC
DATE	TUESDAY 7 AUGUST 2012, KO 7.45PM
VENUE	IBROX STADIUM
ATTENDANCE	38,160
SCORE	4-0

Some Views from the Fans

David Edgar, age 34, web man

CLUB *Rangers.*

SEASON TICKET *Yes.*

FIRST GAME

Rangers v Dundee Utd, 1986.

BEST MEMORY

Helicopter Sunday.

WORST MEMORY

Losing UEFA Cup Final.

BEST FOOTBALL QUOTE

'I'd hang myself, but we can't afford the rope' – Iain Munro as Hamilton manager.

IS THE BAW BURST?

F***, yeah.

How will the situation at Rangers affect Scottish football?
It sucks money out of the game, and it's hardened attitudes. It's shown the game to be corrupt, agenda-driven and filled with hate.

If it's held a mirror up to Scottish football, then the results aren't pretty.

Will the 'new' Rangers differ from the liquidated company or is it business as usual albeit in a different league?
It solely depends on whether you want it to or not. I'm a Rangers fan, we're playing at Ibrox, we're Rangers. End of.

The 'new' Rangers are plying their trade in Division Three. Was this the right decision?
Yes. Clubs can't be allowed to liquidate and start again debt-free without there being a handicap for doing so.

What does the future hold for Rangers and Celtic, assuming Rangers make it back to the top tier of Scottish football?
We'll be fine. This has made us realise how we'd taken our club for granted. It's also created a unity among the support, a real siege mentality. Couldn't care less about Celtic.

As for the other clubs in Scotland, for the SFL clubs we will, as a support, do our best to help them in any way we can. As for the SPL clubs, one day we'll have a chance to do them a bad turn... and we'll do it with a smile on our face.

What do we need to do to improve Scottish football?
Stop it being run by idiots and bigots would be a start.

Andrew Gordon, age 53, quantity surveyor

CLUB *Aberdeen.*

SEASON TICKET *Yes.*

FIRST GAME

I think it was a friendly against Chelsea in 1966.

BEST MEMORY

At Pittodrie, beating Bayern Munich 3-2 in the QF of the Cup Winners Cup in March 1983.

WORST MEMORY

Can't remember, too many!

BEST FOOTBALL QUOTE

Unprintable I'm afraid. But I'll go for 'There's only two Andy Gorams'.

IS THE BAW BURST?

Yes.

How will the situation at Rangers affect Aberdeen Football Club?
Aberdeen, like Celtic, will miss the rivalry of playing Rangers. Commercially, television deals aside, Aberdeen will need to put 647 fans into each home game to make up for the 11,000 Rangers fans that will not attend. I think this will happen, particularly given the low attendance figures of the last few seasons. Also, assuming the greater likelihood of success without Rangers, this will probably be exceeded and overall attendances will increase this season. We will see.

How will the situation at Rangers affect Scottish football?
Rangers will be back in the SPL within three years; of this I have no doubt.

On their way through the league structure they will positively benefit, commercially, each of the lower league clubs.

I don't know the television deal situation and this is crucial to answering this from an SPL commercial perspective. However, I think it will make the SPL more interesting for the non-Old Firm supporters (after all, dominance by one team is only slightly more tedious than dominance by two teams).

Ultimately, in three years' time normal service will be resumed and Scottish football will still be in the same state as it's in now.

Scottish football needs a strong Aberdeen. Why have they struggled so much in recent years?
This would need a thesis in itself:

- Lack of vision and leadership. This was something that Aberdeen had in abundance during their successful years.
- Lack of investment, although it is recognised where this might lead in terms of living above one's means.
- Sky TV and the resulting affluence of the English leagues (this has greatly affected the Old Firm also).
- Undoubtedly the emergence in 1986 of Rangers as a 'big spending club' (Aberdeen were second to Rangers five times in their 'nine in a row' I think). Aberdeen suffered more than most because of this policy by trying to keep up. The game in Scotland had changed forever and ultimately even Rangers could not sustain it because of the subsequent arrival of my second point, above. Perhaps some sanity will now return but we are always left with the satellite TV situation.
- Not identifying and picking up the best of the emerging young players as had been the case in the '60s and '70s.
- Not capitalising on the success of the '80s by harnessing the undoubted wealth of the north-east business community.
- The Bosman ruling (obviously not unique to Aberdeen).

What do we need to do to improve Scottish football?
That's a hard one. I will first outline what I think is and has gone wrong with Scottish football at both club and international level. I've been following Scottish football for a long time. I've seen various restructurings and it always seems to have been ultimately about change for change's sake. It's the expectation that if you change things somehow it will get better but both our international team's and clubs' standings prove without doubt that we have been on a steady decline over the past 30 years or so, despite all the 'restructuring'. There are many reasons for this:

- Other countries have got better at playing football (the Scandinavians for example).
- The utterly disproportionate amount of money available to the English league clubs.
- The break-up of the eastern block suddenly resulting in the emergence of about another twenty 'half-decent' footballing nations (including club sides).
- For some reason the Scottish players by comparison to other nations

have not improved and have, in my view, declined generally in ability.
- The dominance of the Old Firm.
- At international level, players picking and choosing their games, i.e. too big for the team.
- Perhaps the over-use of (average) foreign players by our club sides. It's an interesting statistic that three Scottish clubs have won European trophies and all were achieved with (I think) 100 per cent home-grown players.

We can't do anything about the first three issues, but perhaps we can about the rest (although some will prove very hard).

Other comments
Scottish football is horribly skewed by the dominance of the Old Firm.

I obtained a ticket for the author for The Rangers FC's first league game of the 2012/2013 season at Balmoor. I pointed out to the seller that it was in the home section and that the author was a Rangers supporter. 'Oh that won't matter,' he said, 'it'll be half-full of Rangers fans anyway, there's hundreds of them in Peterhead.'

The dominance of the Old Firm means that every Saturday there are thousands of people driving past their local football stadiums to support either Rangers or Celtic. This is ultimately why there is such animosity between Aberdeen and Rangers (95 per cent of people in the north-east who don't support a local team support Rangers).

It would be a positive thing for Scottish football if the current demise and rebirth of Rangers meant that even just a few of their fans reconsidered their approach and helped to start a rebalancing of Scottish football.

Alison Fletcher, age 50, biomedical scientist (retired)

CLUB *Rangers.*

SEASON TICKET *Yes.*

FIRST GAME

Late 1960.

BEST MEMORY

Being in Florence the night we beat Fiorentina to reach the UEFA Cup final, 2008.

WORST MEMORY

Losing 4-1 at home to unknown Romanian side Unirea.

BEST FOOTBALL QUOTE

'Keep the high balls low.'

IS THE BAW BURST?

YES!

How will the situation at Rangers affect Scottish football?
The loss of the money generated by Rangers will lead to major financial hardship for SPL clubs.

Will the 'new' Rangers differ from the liquidated company, or is it business as usual, albeit in a different league?
Rangers remain the same club. Charles Green bought and paid for the history.

The 'new' Rangers are plying their trade in Division Three. Was this the right decision?
Yes. We had no right to be in the top division. We have to earn that right by working our way back up the leagues.

What does the future hold for Rangers and Celtic, assuming Rangers make it back to the top tier of Scottish football?
In financial terms Rangers will get stronger, Celtic will become weaker.

What do we need to do to improve Scottish football?
Regionalise the smaller teams to cut their costs. Cut ticket prices. Stop

changing match dates and kick-off times to suit TV at the detriment of fans who attend games.

Other comments

Scottish football is in a dire position. Our national team is very poor both in skill levels and tactical awareness. Our club sides are pathetic in European competitions. The whole game needs completely overhauled at all levels.

3

PETERHEAD V RANGERS

Balmoor Blues

IT WAS FRIDAY night and I was setting the alarm. Yes, I would be up early on my beloved Saturday and the usual routine would be abandoned. And the reason – Saturday 11 August 2012 was the start of the Scottish Football League season and I would be travelling to Balmoor Stadium for the Third Division clash between Peterhead and Rangers. The serious business of winning the league and therefore promotion was about to begin. All of a sudden, the early morning wake up call didn't seem so bad. Feelings of anticipation, excitement and bewilderment were all flying through me. A new journey had begun and I wondered how this unique season would unfold.

I left Prestwick just after 8am and was in the north-east harbour town before midday. The journey up had been amusing. Every other lay-by north of Perth had groups of Rangers fans studying the flora at the roadside! These boys had obviously been on the beer from early in the morning, which was understandable. Finally they could get back to supporting their team and forget about all of the other nonsense that had plagued the club in recent months. The police were also highly visible on the approaches to the town. Hopefully they weren't expecting any trouble but you never know. Four or five hours on a bus with nothing to do but drink can be a problem. Add to the mix the ill-feeling towards the Scottish Football Association and the bitterness of being ejected from the top league and suddenly you have a nasty cocktail. Much to think about. My mood brightened when I noticed the Peterhead sign with a Gers scarf wrapped around it. Welcome to Peterhead and Division Three.

The sat-nav took me right up to the stadium and I was keen to have a look. On my last visit I parked in the stadium car park but

I had a feeling that this trip would be a wee bit different. And it was. The place was mobbed and it was an hour before kick-off. Outside broadcast units and other service vehicles completely dominated the area outside the main stand. Police cones were laid out on the main road and side streets. People were out in their gardens waving flags and photographers were everywhere. The hi-viz brigade were directing the proceedings and fans mingled in groups taking it all in. What a contrast from my last visit in April 2011. Peterhead went down to the Third Division after a 2-0 defeat to East Fife that day as 473 fans watched a spirited but futile attempt to stay in the Second Division. At that final whistle in 2011, I sensed almost relief from some of the fans. The season was over, now they could start afresh – a bit like Rangers today. I turned around and went back towards the town. I parked on Catto Drive and headed into Morrisons to use the conveniences. The place was full of people clad in light blue who'd had the same idea. I walked back out into the sunshine and up Balmoor Terrace to the ground.

Again, I was keen to compare this visit with my previous one and wandered around the stadium taking photographs. I had decided to make contact with fans from other clubs to get their views on the game and telephoned Peterhead stalwart Graeme McLean after I had reached the cordon of stewards at the away end. I'd spoken to him a few days earlier and he was delighted to contribute. We met for the first time just behind the big blue coach that had stopped outside the main entrance. Ally McCoist and his players disembarked to a rapturous reception – they really were in Division Three! Graeme and I exchanged pleasantries and talked football. This was not only a massive day for Rangers, it was for Peterhead as well. Things were beginning to come into perspective. We continued talking until Graeme was called into the office. I stood back and tried to make sense of it all.

I purchased a programme and walked out to the fence at the Astroturf pitch. I was reading through it when I recognised the guy standing next to me smoking. Ian McColl, former player and man-ager, was enjoying a puff and I approached him to get his thoughts on the situation. His conclusion was swift and to the point. 'Lot of pish this, they'll restructure this season and they'll be back [Rangers] in the top league within a couple of seasons'. I had heard about this scenario a few times now. Basically, some of the top teams would struggle fi-nancially without Rangers in their league and would push for change. Bigger leagues would mean that Rangers could be back at the top table

Do they mean Berwick Rangers?

earlier rather than via the present route which would take at least three seasons. I think this one will rumble on. Ian stubbed his cigarette and headed for his seat in the commentary box, I walked up towards the scarf man for a memento.

On the way up I bumped into Gers legend Colin Jackson. We'd met briefly before on STV's *Scotland Tonight* programme in June. Never in our wildest dreams (or nightmares) did we expect to meet again in Peterhead for Rangers opening league game of the season! Colin recalled playing in Peterhead during his career but couldn't quite place the ground. I explained to him that it's a new one. The supermarket that I had visited a few minutes earlier was built on the site of the old one. We chatted briefly for another few minutes before making our way to the entrance. I pulled my ticket from my pocket and clicked through the turnstile. Welcome to Division Three.

Officially, I was in the home end but you couldn't tell. The Blue Toon faithful have colours similar to their Glaswegian counterparts and everyone just blended into the mix. My first port of call was the snack bar. I had stopped en route at McDonalds for a breakfast but it was close to lunchtime and I was peckish again. I thought back to my last visit to this outlet and decided to get chips and a Bovril – couldn't face another of those 'hybrid' pie things! As usual the service was good and the two items cost a reasonable £2.70. Add the £12 ticket and £2 programme and it's just under £17, which I think is about right for an hour and a half of football. OK, my fuel cost would be significant but

43

that's primarily because I'm on my own. If I'd taken a supporter's bus it would have been cheaper. Supporting Rangers this season will be more affordable for more people and that can only be a good thing.

The atmosphere was building nicely as kick-off time approached. Most of the noise was coming from the Gers fans and I noticed numerous people moving away from the crescendo of noise that surrounded me. I was in amongst hundreds of Rangers fans who had taken over the Peterhead end of the stadium. Some were a bit miffed at losing their usual spots but the majority (many of whom were clad in dual Peterhead/Rangers scarves) were enjoying the occasion. The singing was loud and the bouncing got wilder as the teams emerged. So much so that one of the fittings on the temporary scaffold gave way – here we go!

A couple of minutes later (12.45pm) SFL season 2012/13 kicked off on a beautiful summer's day. From the first kick of the ball everything that had happened over the past few months was forgotten. The Peterhead lads rose to the occasion and gave their illustrious visitors the baptism of fire that their vice-chairman Ian Grant had craved – welcome to the real fitba. And what a game of football it was. Rangers dominated in the early stages and took the lead through youngster Barrie McKay. Many, myself included, thought that this would signal a goal rush. This wasn't the case and the hosts were unlucky to go in one down at half time. The second half was as frantic as the first and Peterhead got the equaliser they deserved 20 minutes after the break. The almost perfect surface was helping the players produce some good football and the much talked about gulf between the teams was non-existent – this was an excellent contest from start to finish.

And what a finish it was. Peterhead deservedly took the lead with about eight minutes to go. There was disbelief amongst the thousands of Rangers fans. This was supposed to be a fresh start. Victory would be the catalyst for rebuilding the club yet here we were facing humiliation at the very first hurdle. This wasn't in the script! With seconds to spare, Rangers equalised. The place erupted in a communal sigh of relief. A point on the road isn't that bad after all!

The place was slow in emptying after the final whistle but it wasn't too long before I was back in the car and heading south. What a day it had been and we still had all the other games to look forward to. I had to decline an invitation for a cup of tea with Graeme (my wife was planning a BBQ) to talk more about Scottish football. I paused and thought about how the Blue Toon faithful would be feeling after that –

Peterhead would be even livelier than normal tonight!

On the Ball was my choice of listening for the journey home and I was interested to hear of the attendances at the SPL games. I mentioned in Volume 1 of *Is The Baw Burst?* that if teams like Aberdeen, Hearts, Dundee Utd etc had more chance of winning things then fans would back them. The proof would be in the pudding and I was encouraged by the news that Aberdeen had over 14,000 at Pittodrie. Would this be the case for the rest of the season though? 'Sell out Saturday', a valiant attempt at encouraging fans along to games had strategically been scheduled for when Rangers were playing away from home. The total attendance was just over 40,000 for the five SPL games. Incredibly, Third Division Rangers should get more next week at Ibrox for the East Stirlingshire fixture – funny old game.

I was home before 7pm and, for safety reasons, immediately took control of the BBQ from the better half – women, wine and BBQs don't mix! It had been a long but enjoyable day and it was good to have met up with Graeme. He is very positive about the future for Peterhead and the game in general and provided some very funny quotes. Next up would be East Stirlingshire at Ibrox and I was really looking forward to it – who would have thought?

Quotes of the day – *The Rangers fans, that's all I could hear: 'Ye's only sing when yer fishing, sing when yer fishing!'*

'We're only here for the haddock, here for the haddock, we're only here for the haddock!'

'We've got yer team oan the telly!'

GAME	PETERHEAD VERSUS RANGERS
COMPETITION	SFL3
DATE	SATURDAY 11 AUGUST 2012, KO 12.45PM
VENUE	BALMOOR STADIUM
ATTENDANCE	4,485
SCORE	2-2

Some Views from the Fans

Graeme McLean, age 49, train conductor

CLUB *Peterhead.*

SEASON TICKET *Yes.*

FIRST GAME

Can't remember.

BEST MEMORY

October 1971, as an eight-year-old boy attending my first Scotland game v. Belgium at Pittodrie, we won 1-0, scorer John O'Hare (Derby Co.) and a certain Mr Dalglish making his debut.

WORST MEMORY

Being in Cardiff the night Jock Stein died.

BEST FOOTBALL QUOTES

'We don't do walking away!'
    Love football stories, Bill Shankly used to set up subutteo games at training to show his players tactics. Against Man. Utd he had the teams set up as usual and systematically went through their team pointing out their weaknesses and removing them from the table. At the end he had three players left; Best, Law & Charlton. A Liverpool player stated, 'You've three left, boss,' to which Shankly replied, 'If my team can't beat three f***ing players then you're no team o' mine.'
    Also loved seeing banners at games, mainly finals and internationals but these are now sadly disappearing. Favourites that spring to mind – Scotland v England at Hampden; 'Jesus saves, but Kenny nets the rebound' and a 1980s cup final, Aberdeen v Rangers; 'John McMaster lays on more balls than Emmanuel'.

IS THE BAW BURST?

Not at all, but it does have a manageable leak. Saturday's games (11/08/12) showed there are signs of recovery. Hopefully the powers that be take notice and help rather than hinder. 14,000 at Pittodrie for a game against Ross Co. was a superb attendance and I have also noticed East Stirlingshire's crowds have been in the region of 500 which is double their usual gate last season.

How will the situation at Rangers affect Peterhead Football Club?
Rangers are where they deserve to be AS A NEW CLUB. If CVA had been accepted then remaining in the SPL would have been appropriate, but the whole situation should have been handled better by the SFA. They went into administration on 14 February. In my view, given time to evaluate, a laid down procedure should have been stated by end of April as to what might happen in various scenarios. Being left to July, hoping other people would make decisions was pathetic. The transfer embargo is wrong in its present form, if Rangers are not allowed to sign players for one year, I feel that they should be allowed to start signing players from 15 February 2013, one year after entering administration, not from 1 September 2012 as it presently is. Also, as CVA was rejected, why should new Rangers still be accountable for old Rangers debts? It wouldn't happen in any other industry.

How will the situation at Rangers affect Scottish football?
'I think at the end of the day the Rangers situation will be good for Scottish football, it proves no single club is bigger than the system in that there are consequences to actions carried out by those representing clubs. The smaller clubs will benefit in the short term by increased revenue from increased gates and all that comes with that (bar, shop takings etc), but ultimately it proves Rangers are only another club and have the same responsibilities as everyone else. Welcome to the Third Division!'

I've tried to work from memory for the answer I would have put at the start of the season, the only difference now being I've since been made aware that Third Division clubs are only to receive a one-off payment of £10,000 for televising games whether they host Sky/BBC once or both their home games against Rangers. With increased costs involved this wipes out any benefit from monies received. It is a scenario Peterhead may possibly find themselves in as their January clash may well be a top-of-the-table encounter.

Peterhead FC has a good infrastructure in place, why are they languishing in Division Three?
Why are Peterhead in Division Three? No easy answer here, you could say we were unlucky, things didn't go our way, which is true but after a while it became a confidence thing as we got into the losing habit. Poor selection of managers didn't help, but in Jim McInally we have learned from that error and are definitely making progress. Although John Sheran was/is a nice guy he just wasn't the right man for the job at that time.

What do we need to do to improve Scottish football?

What needs to be done is not a simple answer, something involving ALL 42 clubs, not a decision based on two or three main clubs' benefit. Personally for me, a 16-team top league giving a 30-game season playing each other only twice, perhaps having the League Cup in a small league format, seeded so there is one 'big' team in each league, ideally eight leagues so eight top teams would form quarter-final stages then traditional knock-out thereafter. Maybe even regionalise these early stages for financial considerations.

Other comments

On the whole we now have a fantastic opportunity to totally restructure our beloved game but no rash decisions should be taken. A committee should be formed with people like Henry McLeish, Andy Roxburgh, past players like John Grieg and Billy McNeill and a referee representative like John Rowbotham to look at the game from ALL angles. We want the next hundred years to be successful and the right decisions should be made for clubs to move forward, but one thing is for certain: one club, one vote must be implemented, with a majority of no less than 60 per cent being required to enforce changes.

These are personal opinions gathered from watching from afar and bar-room boardrooms thinking we could do better than them!

Jim McMahon, age 63, director

CLUB *Motherwell.*

SEASON TICKET *Yes.*

FIRST GAME
Motherwell v Airdrie, 1954.

BEST MEMORY
Cup win 1991, games with my dad.

WORST MEMORY
Losing to Rangers – semi-final 1976.

BEST FOOTBALL QUOTE
'He's slower than he looks' – Bill Shankly on Tony Hateley.

IS THE BAW BURST?
No.

How will the situation at Rangers affect Motherwell Football Club?
Less than we originally anticipated – the TV money has been maintained at about the same level, but the loss of a home game is about £125k per match.

How will the situation at Rangers affect Scottish football?
Hopefully will invigorate it with new options and less Old Firm 'rubbish'.

Motherwell FC has experienced administration. What has the club learned from that situation?
Never to go there again, but easy to say and hard to do.
   Any Premier club which finishes in the bottom six has huge cash flow problems.
   March–May – engage with fans as we did in our money raising round.

Motherwell, St Johnstone, Hearts and Dundee United have all been eliminated from Europe in their first round of matches. How can we improve on this dismal annual statistic?
Really wish I knew – needs more money from local business/community to find and hang onto better players a bit longer. If we manage that, one or more teams could go through.

What do we need to do to improve Scottish football?
More young Scottish talent playing in our leagues – reawaken the romance of the game again.

4

RANGERS V EAST STIRLINGSHIRE

Memories

GAME 4 OF THE LATEST *Is The Baw Burst?* journey was a Saturday afternoon trip to Ibrox. The Gers hosted East Stirlingshire in their first home league match of the season in another unique day in this remarkable campaign. It was also a special day for me. On that day 30 years previously, I started work along the road in Govan Shipbuilders and to celebrate I would be meeting up with a former colleague (who is also a lifelong Teddy Bear) after the game. Football and football talk over a few beers – perfect.

The post match arrangements meant that I was travelling by train and I settled down with the earphones in and started from the back of the Saturday paper. My usual trawl through the football sections was interrupted by texts from my niece. She informed me that she was going to her first game at Ibrox with her friend and her friend's parents. Excellent. The situation at the new Rangers was definitely capturing people's attention and, as I mentioned in previous chapters, it's now so much more affordable for your average family. Hopefully many more youngsters would attend over the coming months and get the bug for the football.

The newspapers were still featuring the Ian Black story. The new Rangers midfielder made his Scotland debut, against Australia, to a chorus of boos at Easter Road in midweek. The coverage had dominated the week's football news – what else could they write about it! There were various theories as to why this happened. The two most prominent ones related to the fact that he played for the Hearts side that had humbled Hibs in the Scottish Cup Final a few months ago, and that he had signed for Rangers. I feel it was probably a combination of the two but, whatever the reason, it's totally unacceptable. I still

Then, now, forever.

cringe when I think back to that Parkhead night when Gary McAllister was mercilessly booed by his own supporters. Hopefully the Easter Road boo boys will come to their senses.

As the train passed Ibrox Stadium I started thinking about the Rangers team of 1982. Back then we were in the doldrums, hanging onto the coat tails of Celtic and the New Firm. How things have changed! The highlights in those days were Scottish and League Cup runs but at least we had a decent stadium. Then, in April 1986, just as my apprenticeship was reaching its conclusion, Graeme Souness arrived and turned Scottish football on its head. I was a main stand regular in those days and I'll never forget the first home game of season 1986/87. Dundee United beat us 3-2 but it was the size of the crowd that day that sticks in my memory. I was lucky to have a seat, unlike the hundreds, maybe thousands, who were stuck standing in aisles and at the top of stairs.

Rangers changed significantly under Souness, never more obviously than the day when he signed Maurice Johnston. I can still vividly remember that day in 1989 in the shipyard. One of the apprentices came running up to me and told me to get to a radio for the 11am bulletin on Radio Clyde as Mo would be signing for the Gers. I didn't believe him but managed to tune in anyway and sure enough, he'd signed. Looking back now, it really was incredible!

That was just the beginning of a wonderful, trophy-laden journey that you eventually took for granted. Scottish dominance, trailblazers in the Champions League and leaders in all the associated marketing and hospitality paraphernalia that's synonymous with top level football today. Former chairman David Murray is due credit for enabling such a transformation, I just wonder if we'll ever really know why and where it all went wrong. I have a suspicion that *credit* is the root cause!

I left Central Station and headed for the subway. I was early, so I disembarked at Cessnock and walked along to Edmiston Drive where I purchased a match programme. In his match notes, manager Ally McCoist spoke of a new chapter in the club's history. It was the first time that a Third Division match would take place at Ibrox. Ok, it was far removed from the trailblazing realms of yesteryear, but it was still a first and for football fans the world over it is these kind of sentimental issues that pulls them back every week. And the fans were back in huge numbers, more than 49,000 of them. Many, myself included, with a spring in their step. It was a new beginning, why not be positive and enjoy it?

My mate Robbie arrived, late as usual, and we headed up into the stand. The place was filling up nicely and the PA system was blaring out the old favourites.

The teams emerged to rapturous applause, completed the formalities and we settled down for the game. Within three minutes, the Shire were 1-0 up. You couldn't make this stuff up! The hundred or so East Stirlingshire faithful were on cloud nine. They had taken the lead away from home in the biggest game in their history – brilliant! Rangers did eventually come back and win comfortably, but I can guarantee that the Shire faithful will talk about that penalty for years to come. And that's what it's all about – supporting your team through the highs and the lows.

The game was again entertaining and for the Ibrox faithful five goals will always go down well. I felt the Shire boys had done OK. They weren't overawed, nor were they humiliated and I'm sure they all thoroughly enjoyed their day out at Ibrox. I too had enjoyed the first three games of the season. There was a freshness to the proceedings and at last we had been relieved of the endless drudgery of the SPL. Game over – time for beer.

I left Robbie and strolled along to meet my 'old' mate Keith in the Old Toll Bar. We were soon in deep conversation about the last 30 years but the banter quickly and inevitably moved on to Rangers. He had had his season ticket for 27 years and was deeply upset at the liquidation of the club, whereas I had mellowed slightly over the last few weeks. The embarrassment of the situation is still uncomfortable but at the end of the day Rangers are still Rangers. That would never change. OK, we are in Division Three and will be away from football's top table for the foreseeable future, but you need bad times in order to really appreciate the good times. We may as well get on with it in a positive and respectful manner.

After a rapid few pints we headed for the city centre to catch up with Robbie again. We talked football, and drank, until it was getting difficult to understand each other and then went our separate ways.

A few days later, I spoke with Shiretrust chairman Ian Fleming. He described his day at Ibrox as 'amazing'. Wined and dined and treated with total respect, and of course his 'wee' team took the lead against the fallen giants. I enquired about the return leg at Ochilview and how they would handle the big crowd. He assured me that planning was already underway and the club would do its utmost to ensure a great day out for the travelling support. It's one I was already looking forward too.

Quote of the day – *Rangers fan just after the Shire's penalty award: 'Do these Third Division referees no know that ye don't gie penalties at Ibrox?'*

GAME	RANGERS VERSUS EAST STIRLINGSHIRE
COMPETITION	SFL 3
DATE	SATURDAY 18 AUGUST 2012, KO 3PM
VENUE	IBROX STADIUM
ATTENDANCE	49,118
SCORE	5-1

Some Views from the Fans

Frank Meade, age 62, football club chairman

CLUB *Albion Rovers.*

SEASON TICKET *Yes.*

FIRST GAME *1961.*

BEST MEMORY

Winning the Second Division play-off in 2011 to gain promotion, and again in 2012 to remain in Division Two.

WORST MEMORY

Too many to list!

BEST FOOTBALL QUOTE

The more I watch football the less I know about it!

IS THE BAW BURST?

No.

How will the situation at Rangers affect Albion Rovers Football Club?
Our club will be hit financially by losing the income from our two derby matches against Airdrie United. That's about eight per cent of our income. The major challenge for us is to stay in Division Two and sustain our revenue streams.

How will the situation at Rangers affect Scottish football?
I think there will be a dumbing down of standards in the medium term but that should encourage clubs to play more young players in their first teams. In the short term it's about survival and it's important that we don't press the panic button at this stage.

What does the future hold for a club like Albion Rovers?
I'd like to think that we will grow into being a sustainable Division Two club which will have a broad appeal to the people of Coatbridge. The most important thing, though, is that the club survives in the long term and that our supporters continue to enjoy their football.

Inverness CT and Ross County have made it to the SPL from the Highland League. What's stopping the Wee Rovers making it to the top tier of Scottish football?
A lack of investment in the club over a long period of time coupled with facing competition from Glasgow's big two clubs.

What do we need to do to improve Scottish football?
We need to keep developing young players. Our job in football is to help every child achieve his or her potential. I feel that the concentration on elite youngsters will narrow the game's base and reduce participation at all levels of the game. Also we should look at making more use of the summer months by starting the season earlier and having a winter shutdown.

Other comments
There is still much to celebrate about Scottish football and we need to make sure that we get the good news stories out there rather than giving the doom and gloom merchants lots of airtime.

Keith MacDonald, age 42, civil engineer

CLUB   *Heart of Midlothian FC.*

SEASON TICKET   *No.*

FIRST GAME

Hearts v Kilmarnock 1971, aged two (my dad says I fell asleep on the barrier, halfway through the first half).

BEST MEMORY

4,000 Hearts fans walking through Bordeaux before a UEFA Cup game. Atmosphere terrific, locals came out to meet us, and swap scarves etc, then we won the game 1-0 thanks to Marc De Vries' header! It doesn't get much better. AND Beating Rangers 2-1 in the Scottish Cup Final 1998, to end our 40 year wait for the trophy.

WORST MEMORY

Losing to Airdrie in cup semis in the 1990s twice!

BEST FOOTBALL QUOTE

'You don't win anything wi kids' – Hansen.

IS THE BAW BURST?

No.

How will the situation at Rangers affect Heart of Midlothian Football Club?

Losing the two Rangers games will obviously affect turnover through the gate, especially as Rangers will be replaced by Dundee, who may not fill the away end. Plus the money received from Sky will reduce. It has, however, removed one half of the Auld Firm, which allows Hearts to challenge Celtic for the Champions League positions. Hearts (Mr Romanov) were already looking to reduce the playing staff and the wage bill, as we were paying over the odds for players, and had too many on the books.

We are now concentrating on bringing through the young players, from the Academy at Riccarton, which is the obvious way forward. This, coinciding with Rangers' relegation to the Third Division, may be difficult in the short term, but will benefit Hearts in the long term.

How will the situation at Rangers affect Scottish football?

The reduced revenue from the TV deal and the potential loss of possibly two Rangers home games will force the other teams in the SPL to look at their finances more closely. Playing squads will have to reduce, with clubs looking to take players on loan, and on free transfers. The clubs will be unable to compete with comparable clubs in the English lower leagues, which may further reduce the quality of player on view in Scottish football. The amount of money on offer to players, even Celtic, may prohibit players from coming to Scottish football.

In the SFL, the Third Division teams will benefit greatly financially by the two visits of Rangers to their grounds, plus the players themselves will enjoy going to Ibrox for the away games. As long as the Rangers support keeps interest in visiting the smaller grounds through the winter periods, there should be short term gain in the SFL Third Division, and if Rangers do win promotion, the Second and First Division teams will also benefit.

Hearts currently have high levels of debt. Can this debt be reduced or does another Rangers scenario loom?
Reduce the playing squad dramatically, and get rid of the high earners. Hearts had over 55 players in the first team and reserves last year. This needs to reduce to concentrate on bring the younger players through the Academy, with a scattering of senior experienced players. This is how Hearts came through in the early 1980s under Alec MacDonald and Sandy Jardine, to become a force again in Scottish football. The priority must be to develop players and sell them on to England, where at present money, especially in the EPL, is no option. Look at Blackburn paying £8 million for Jordan Rhodes.

The worry is that Mr Romanov gets bored and wants out. However, he has already placed a £50 million price tag for Hearts, which would scare any potential investors or takeovers, so if he did want out, he would surely have a more sensible value of HMFC to get them off his hands.

The stadium situation remains on the agenda – what's the answer?
The answer is to redevelop the main stand to give Hearts a purpose-built 23–25,000 stand, with more hospitality capacity, for increased revenue.

Scotland needs a stadium with low–mid 20,000 capacity for semi-finals without the Old Firm in them. However, due to the current planning problems in getting the new stand approved, and the current financial situation at Hearts, this is still on the back burner.

What we need is a Russian billionaire, to throw money at it. We only have a Russian millionaire!

Tynecastle is the spiritual home of HMFC. A move away from Tynecastle has its risks. Whilst making it easier for away fans from the West and

North to get to the game, would people from Edinburgh go the outskirts to watch football?

Removing Hearts from Gorgie Road would also affect the local community and especially hostelries.

A move to the outskirts to a purpose-built stadium, for football, rugby, athletics, pop concerts etc with greater hospitality provision would boost income, and the way forward may be to co-fund with Edinburgh City Council, who know that Meadowbank is now archaic, and needs renewal. The traffic links are getting better, with the construction of the trams out to Gogar, so the infrastructure is getting better.

What do we need to do to improve Scottish football?
- Keep the SPL at maximum of 12. Anything more would lead to more meaningless games.
- Get the prices reduced. We need to realise that £40 for a game is too much.
- Summer football is a must, played from March to October. Our climate is changing dramatically, with wetter conditions throughout. People would go to games throughout the summer months more readily if the viewing conditions were better, played on better pitches.
- Summer football has obviously benefited Scandinavian countries, who we used to beat readily, but who now have a better rating in European football than us.

Other comments
If Rangers have been 'at it' with dual contracts, it is right that they are stripped of their trophies during the period concerned.

5

BERWICK RANGERS V RANGERS

Dunbarrassing

GAME 5 OF THE TOUR had been planned well in advance. When the fixture list was published, I immediately pencilled in Berwick, as well as Annan, as family weekend trips if tickets were available. Thankfully, one of my contacts managed to produce the brief and Shielfield Park was a reality. We had settled on a caravan site in Dunbar and set off late on Friday evening. About three hours later, after numerous U-turns, dead ends and emptying the boot to get a 'real' paper map book (wife was navigating), we arrived at the site. By the time we had set up the caravan and had some food and a few beers it was time for bed.

Saturday was spent walking on the coast and enjoying the many attractions that Dunbar has to offer. A fish supper, obligatory when visiting a seaside town, was our choice of evening meal. The food was excellent and we had had a very enjoyable day. This is what being a football fan is all about, I reflected whilst opening a cold beer. Prior to a game, I usually do some forward planning but this time, no internet meant that I would be relying on the knowledge gained from the last trip. The plan was for the wife, Debbi, to drop me off at the stadium and she would head off and do the coastal walk that she had enjoyed on our last visit. And it worked a treat! After breakfast on Sunday morning, we headed south for Rangers' first competitive league match in England.

It took us just over half an hour to get to the stadium. En route, Debbi was amazed by the amount of minibuses in lay-bys. 'What are they doing?' she enquired. 'Probably having a quick smoke!' I replied. I was taken aback by the amount of police on duty. They were everywhere. What were they expecting? OK, there is always a risk but to have them at every other lay-by and junction was a bit over

Horses as well.

the top. And it was worse outside the ground. Horses and motorbikes patrolled the adjacent streets and there were stewards everywhere – it was 11.30am on Sunday morning, for heaven's sake! Yes, some would have been on the sauce from early doors but it was never likely to be another Manchester!

After agreeing a pick up point with Debbi, I made my way through the crowds of police and stewards and into the away end at Shielfield. The place was busy and my first choice vantage point was immediately dismissed due to the risk of tumbling backwards down the steep slope. Under the canopy was too busy as well, so I decided to head towards the periphery at the Etal Road end. First though, I needed to use the toilets and waited in the massive queue leading to the old wooden building. Like many, I couldn't wait and reluctantly headed for the back of the hut. These old grounds might be spacious but most don't have the facilities that are required nowadays. The standing areas are also lacking. Grassy slopes are not suitable underfoot conditions.

Enough moaning, time to enjoy the football on another beautiful summer's day. It really was scorching and I was worried about the old napper getting sunburnt but there was nothing I could do. Others were less concerned and there were loads of bare chests dotted about the place. These daring supporters also revealed much about their loyalties and commitment to various causes. Many had tattoos depicting, amongst other things, famous battles from years gone by and declarations of how they will continue the fight. I really wish that we could move on from this stuff. It drags the club down. Now is the perfect opportunity to go forward positively. Focus on the great things that this club has achieved over the years and build on that for the future. The sectarian issues are tiresome and suffocating and everyone must work together to eradicate them.

Back to the football, and the teams got started on a lush but bumpy looking pitch. I was struggling to see properly and continually bobbed about trying to take in the action. Hundreds of wasps were also accountable for this perpetual motion as they buzzed around everyone – it was horrible. Some of the happier chaps didn't even notice them – the cigarette smoke and smell of alcohol must have put them off. I think the Rangers players may have been affected as well because they couldn't string two passes together. The Borderers were enjoying their biggest day for years and getting stuck into their illustrious visitors. I had a feeling before the season began that away games would be problematic for the Glasgow giants, and so far this certainly seemed to be the case. Rangers dominated long spells but failed to turn their superiority into gilt-edged chances. At least the fans were enjoying it. The masses underneath the corrugated shed sang their hearts out (for the entire match). They were loving it. On the stroke of half-time, Rangers took the lead and the place erupted. Should make for an interesting second half, I thought.

As usual, my attention during the break turned to the programme. Page five featured the league table and it was another reminder of where The Rangers really are at the moment. Some of the fans around me were saying how much they were enjoying the day and the situation that the club was in. I was too, to an extent, but wondered how long this newfound enjoyment would last. It would be a different story here in February, of that I have no doubt. Standing outside in poor weather isn't pleasant and unfortunately, many Third Division clubs have little else to offer. But it was pleasant today and therefore I was surprised by the amount of people who left at half-time to go and watch the rest of the game in the pub! Some supporters would have given their left leg for a ticket to this game – on the new journey and all that stuff. Surely they could have stayed off the drink for an hour and a half? Obviously not.

The second half started brightly and, to the delight of the home support, Berwick deservedly equalised. Yes, a team full of international players was being held, and at times outplayed, by a bunch of part-timers. This wasn't in the script. I wondered if the Rangers players had yet to fully understand the situation that they were in. These 'wee' teams were not going to lie down and let the big boys have it all their own way. They would need to scrap and fight for everything in this league and at this moment in time it wasn't happening. Hopefully over the next couple of weeks it would sink in, as this would be no cakewalk.

An increasingly agitated away support was relieved when the referee sounded the whistle for full time. Another two points dropped on the road but it could and should have been much worse. That was the poorest game I'd seen in a while but never mind, let's enjoy the rest of the day. A text message confirmed that Debbi was at the agreed rendezvous point and I headed for the car. I was a bit miffed to have missed out on the bag of chips that I'd promised myself from the van after my last visit. It was in its usual spot next to the main stand but because of the segregation all I got was a whiff every now and again. As I walked back to the car I was happy that we would be back at the caravan site and be able to enjoy the rest of the day – which we did.

An hour later I had a beer in my hand as I tended the BBQ. This was the life. OK, the game was terrible but the overall experience was right up there and this backs up my argument for changing the months in which we play football. I've already mentioned that the next league visit to Berwick is in February and it is not one I'm looking forward to for a number of reasons. The playing surface will not be of the same standard, fans will be making the long journey home in the dark and if the weather is bad then many will be exposed to the elements at Shielfield. Doesn't sound too appealing, does it? Lifelong Berwick supporter David Cook agrees: 'One of the things I'd like to see introduced is summer football. That would benefit teams like Berwick, who wouldn't have to compete with the northeast [of England] giants for local support, and we'd also benefit from being a popular holiday destination, which would lead to an increase in gates. From a spectator's point of view, I'd prefer watching a game on a summer's night to freezing my balls off at Links Park in January.' Thankfully, the BBQ was keeping mine warm and it was still August!

Today's game was the last league game before the transfer window shut on Rangers for 12 months. The remaining 'big' names were disappearing faster than the fans of most SPL clubs. Rumour had it that Captain America Carlos Bocanegra would be next and a threadbare squad would be weakened further. How would the team fare when the inevitable injuries and suspensions kick in? Would the young players cope physically with the sustained challenge? And, most importantly, would the fans put up with it? Only time will tell – the journey continues...

Quote of the day – *Topless Gers fan who spoke continually to a policeman throughout the first half: 'Is it the same laws doon here as it is at Ibrox?'*

GAME	BERWICK RANGERS VERSUS RANGERS
COMPETITION	SFL3
DATE	SUNDAY 26 AUGUST 2012, KO 12PM
VENUE	SHIELFIELD PARK
ATTENDANCE	4,140
SCORE	1-1

Some Views from the Fans

David Cook, age 49, local government officer

CLUB *Berwick Rangers.*

SEASON TICKET *No.*

FIRST GAME

Berwick Rangers v Sunderland, pre-season friendly, 1973.

BEST MEMORY

Winning the league in 78/79 and 2006/07.

WORST MEMORY

Relegation, worst team in our history 2007/08.

BEST FOOTBALL QUOTE

'When he wakes up, tell him he's Pelé.'

IS THE BAW BURST?

No.

How will the situation at 'Glasgow' Rangers affect Berwick Rangers Football Club?
Short term, it will give us an unprecedented four league matches against one of the Old Firm. That will not happen again in my lifetime. We've already had the better of a draw at home to Rangers in front of a full house in the summer sun at Shielfield. It's experiences like that which leaven the (much more) regular misery of watching us at Ochilview on a freezing cold February night in front of 250 people. The income from the home matches against Rangers and the media exposure will both be beneficial to Berwick Rangers. In a wider context, the whole town benefits – people staying over, drinking in the pubs, eating in cafes etc. If we get some new trust members or the club generates some more commercial sponsorship as a consequence, then these are things that would probably not have happened had Rangers not been placed in the Third Division.

The relegation seems to have reinvigorated the Rangers support and the people I spoke to seemed to be really enjoying their time in the Third Division, including the chance to visit new towns and grounds. They seemed to view their situation as a welcome break from the endless drudgery of the Premier League.

The one negative aspect I can think of is that we no longer have a chance of winning the Third Division, a bit like when Livingston were demoted several seasons ago (though they failed to beat us that season). We had ambitions of a play-off spot this season – the presence of Rangers makes that less likely now.

Longer term, the impact of Rangers being in the Third Division will have consequences in regard to the allocation of TV monies, which in turn will have an effect on our financial planning for the next three years at least. Berwick are a well-run club from a financial perspective, but money remains tight and any reduction in income will have an impact on our ability to maintain a competitive team.

How will the situation at 'Glasgow' Rangers affect Scottish football?
Depends on the willingness and ability of the authorities/vested interests who govern Scottish football to come up with a fair and robust set of proposals for reorganisation which will have the effect of revitalising Scottish football. I'm not confident that they possess those attributes. Inertia will prevail and the opportunity afforded to the game in Scotland to bring about meaningful restructure which benefits all clubs will be lost. I hope I'm wrong.

My fear is that the desperate self-interest of the SPL and SFL wannabes will end up sidelining teams like Berwick Rangers.

I think Rangers themselves will recover and return to their former strength, this time without the financial criminality. That will not lead to a more competitive league and may simply restore the status quo.

The Wee Rangers played Rangers at home recently. In what ways did this match differ from a 'normal' Third Division fixture?
The buzz around the pre-match build up, media interest and coverage, the size of the crowd, the amount of police on duty, the quality of our performance, the appearance of many locals who couldn't find Shielfield with sat-nav.

What does the future hold for Berwick Rangers and could they do a Ross County?
As I said earlier, we're a well-run club with supporters organisations now represented in the boardroom. My ambitions are a new or revamped stadium, owned by the club rather than a disinterested county council, with a 4G pitch that can be used as an income generator. In terms of where we fit in, promotion to the Second Division, and an ability to compete for

First Division play-offs would be the limit of our capabilities.

We'll never do a Ross County unless there is a miraculous injection of cash – Berwick is one of the lowest-waged areas in England and the money simply isn't there. What we can do is become a competitive club on the pitch operating from good facilities with a dominant position in the local community.

What do we need to do to improve Scottish football?
How long have you got? The McLeish report identified many of the problems and suggested some sensible solutions. Unless the dominance of the Old Firm is reduced – maybe introducing an American-style salary cap, or first-pick arrangement would have an effect, then everything else will be tinkering at the edges.

Other comments
Good luck with the book!

David Fox, age 51, director

CLUB *Motherwell.*

SEASON TICKET *Yes.*

FIRST GAME

Motherwell v Rangers, 1968.

BEST MEMORY

1991 et al. Also Hearts v Well in cup after Phil O'Donnell died. One time when the entire club stood together from manager to fan.

WORST MEMORY

Home v Dundee Utd when Phil collapsed.

BEST FOOTBALL QUOTE

'Football... bloody hell...' Sir Alex.

IS THE BAW BURST?

No.

How will the situation at Rangers affect Motherwell Football Club?
As with the rest of SPL there will be a new normal which will be a downsizing of the present. The good will be greater opportunity for youth and increased competition for Euro places, the bad will be financial risk to the club, no competition for the title and half the opportunities to beat the Old Firm. It will not be plain sailing but Well should survive if fans temper their expectations to what is necessary to protect the club in the long term. The good time charlies may desert in the short term but will come back when normality returns. A pleasure to do without the Old Firm sectarian media circus for a few years, lets us concentrate on football for a change.

How will the situation at Rangers affect Scottish football?
Largely as above but I expect one or two, Hearts/Killie, to go into administration. Motherwell's administration wiped off the debt and was painful at the time, others have not had that luxury. Rangers will come back stronger as they will similarly be debt free which in the long run puts them back into the ascendancy. The Celtic joy division are not looking longer term at that prospect although their directors are. The biggest losers are Celtic and after a year of exhilaration they will become quickly bored. Rangers fans are on a mission (a la well worth saving), Celtic fans are

losing their perspective and will come up with a bump.

Good news for the small clubs who have the opportunity to wipe out long standing debts as a result of Rangers pay day. I know a Brechin director who, thanks to one home game v Rangers, paid the entire wage bill for the season on the first day – a nice bonus for the wee guy.

Motherwell FC has experienced administration. What has the club learned from that situation?
They have mended the Boyle induced ways and as a result have more realistic aspirations. Staying in SPL is the must have, top six is a welcome bonus, Europe, enjoy it while you can. It was a painful lesson but it was best we learned it before the draconian penalties came in to play.

As a Well fan it is not about winning trophies, it is about watching a 16-year-old called James McFadden playing his first tentative games in senior football.

Motherwell, St Johnstone, Hearts and Dundee United have all been eliminated from Europe in their first round of matches. How can we improve on this dismal annual statistic?
Don't know that we can as it is very much finance driven nowadays. Greater emphasis on home grown Scottish talent will help and the demise of Rangers with consequent reductions in revenue for the others will push us that way. In addition it needs sensible budgeting which means we can get away from the 'must sell a player a season to survive' mentality.

What do we need to do to improve Scottish football?
Get rid of Rangers and Celtic. If we balance net income from them compared to the net income if they are not there it will always be greater but without them it will attract a better type of fan, the families, the grannies. The telly will not have Old Firm games as an attractor but the lower telly money will be split more evenly rather than the lion's share going to the old squirm. Net to the other clubs, it won't be much different.

Outcome – greater crowds because more teams have something to play for, no sectarian nonsense driving away the families and the decent fans and more Scottish-based players nurtured from an early stage. You know it makes sense!

Other comments
My job takes me overseas on a regular basis, Oz, Far East, Canada etc. All these countries cast envious eyes on the passion and quality of Scottish

football. Let's not beat ourselves up too much. We will never be La Liga or Serie A or the Premiership, but we still have a lot to be proud of and thankful for.

6

RANGERS V ELGIN CITY

Lazy Sunday Afternoon – Not

IBROX WAS THE VENUE for Game 6 and I was not a happy bunny! I only realised on Thursday night that the game had been moved to Sunday afternoon at the unbelievable kick-off time of 4.30pm. I honestly don't know anybody who would want to go to a game at that time on a Sunday. OK, maybe a one-off on a bank holiday weekend or the like but not a regular league game. My plan was out the window. I had organised a family meal in Glasgow for the Saturday night and my intention was to head into the city centre after the game and meet up with the rest of them. The meal still happened but here I was heading up to Glasgow on the Sunday as well. The fuzzy (red wine) head wasn't helping matters – hopefully the game would make up for it.

This was my third visit to Ibrox this season. The previous two had been really enjoyable and I wondered if the momentum that was building would be sustained. There had been blips when on the road but generally the team had performed well at the 'Big Hoose' and I think that a key factor in these results was the enthusiasm of the fans. The whole atmosphere feels so much lighter, healthier and almost carefree. It was as if a huge weight had been lifted from everybody's shoulders. People were smiling and getting on with supporting their team. We are where we are. Enjoy it! I parked over on Dalkeith St and made my way over the motorway and down to Edmiston Drive. The brisk walk and warm sun seemed to clear the old head and I was soon scanning the various pavement vendors for a scarf for my ten-year-old niece. She had specifically asked for one with 'we are the people' on it. I spotted one which was duly purchased along with a match day programme. A few hours later back at home I emptied my pockets and unraveled the scarf. I got a wee surprise. On the B side was some

The team of '72 wish they were playing.

nonsense about 'build the gallows, build them high' how could I give this to a ten-year-old? When are we going to move on from all of this rubbish? I really do despair at times. At about 4pm, I decided to head in. My mate Robbie was cutting it fine as usual and the old belly was rumbling away – getting near dinnertime. I couldn't resist. A steak pie and Bovril were devoured whilst watching Southampton v Man United on the big TVs. A beer would have gone down a treat as well. I wondered again about the licensing laws – are they different for SFL clubs? Almost time for the action and it suddenly dawned on me that the team we were playing (Elgin City) was higher up in the league than Rangers – bizarre!

I'd missed the midweek encounter with Falkirk due to work commitments. By all accounts the performance was much better than the previous weekend's escapades down in Berwick. Another healthy crowd (26,450) had witnessed the 3-0 win in what would be the captain's last game for a while. Carlos Bocanegra would be joining Spanish side Racing Santander for the rest of the season on loan. It was also the end of the line for Maurice Edu and Kirk Broadfoot who would be heading south, for Stoke and Blackpool respectively. They moved across the border with the best wishes of the fans, having done the honourable thing and transferred their contracts over to the new-co. Rangers might even get a fee for their transfers, unlike those who walked away.

It wasn't all doom and gloom on the transfer front. David Templeton had signed from Hearts with Faure and Argyriou also joining the ranks. There was much furore about Templeton's decision to leave the SPL club and play in the fourth tier of Scottish football. Typically, Ally McCoist stoutly defended the player and had a go at the snipers. 'There were 46,000 reasons to come to this club,' said McCoist after the Elgin game. Some people don't fully understand the pull of the Glasgow giants.

One man who does is Lee McCulloch and he was appointed club captain in place of Carlos. He responded with two goals and an excellent performance in another good game. Elgin scored a superb opening goal – two home league games in a row where the 'wee' team has opened the scoring. Rangers new boy David Templeton responded with a brace and played really well. The referee had a bit of a nightmare and this wasn't the first time I'd noticed this. Now, I don't mean that he was biased towards any of the teams, it was the inconsistency that was irritating. But it all made for an excellent atmosphere for the entire 90 minutes. Good entertainment, plenty of goals and a novel experience for Elgin City – that's what it's all about.

It turned out that the attendance was second only to Newcastle's in the UK and it was the highest over the weekend in Scotland. Getting over 46,015 people to turn up late on a Sunday afternoon for a Third Division clash is remarkable. Who would have thought that this would be the case after the months of agony that Rangers have suffered. I just wonder what the Italian TV channel, who were filming in the famous Louden Tavern, made of it all. Just another weekend in Scottish football. Next up, Serbia at Hampden and not a Rangers player in sight.

Quote of the day – *Rangers fan: 'When did Elgin get city status?' I can only hope his tongue was firmly in his cheek.*

GAME	RANGERS VERSUS ELGIN CITY
COMPETITION	SFL3
DATE	SUNDAY 2 SEPTEMBER 2012, KO 4.30PM
VENUE	IBROX STADIUM
ATTENDANCE	46,015
SCORE	5-1

Some Views from the Fans

Scot van den Akker, age 41, education manager

CLUB *Rangers.*

SEASON TICKET *Yes.*

FIRST GAME

Rangers 1 Hibs 2.

BEST MEMORY

Skol Cup Final, 1986.

WORST MEMORY

Spring 2012.

BEST FOOTBALL QUOTE

'The ball is round.'

IS THE BAW BURST?

Yes.

How will the situation at Rangers affect Scottish football?
Adversely – obviously. There is no serious minded person who believes it can be anything other than a disaster. The game was already careering – out of control – down a dead end. What now?

Will the 'new' Rangers differ from the liquidated company or is it business as usual, albeit in a different league?
Same club... the club is its fans. Do we support a corporate structure? I don't.

The 'new' Rangers are plying their trade in Division Three. Was this the right decision?
Yes. We have no desire to subsidise the SPL while prevented from competing through endless point deductions etc. Let them 'regroup' and let us do the same.

What does the future hold for Rangers and Celtic, assuming Rangers make it back to the top tier of Scottish football?
Same as before... two bald men fighting over a comb.

What do we need to do to improve Scottish football?
I put this together earlier this year for a project I was working on. So how glorious were the glory days? Between 1960 and 1972:

- Rangers won the European Cup Winners Cup and reached another two finals. They also reached a European Cup semi-final and a Fair's Cup semi-final.
- Hibernian reached the European Cup semi-final, as did Dundee (who also reached a Fair's Cup semi-final)... Kilmarnock and Dunfermline reached the Fair's Cup semi-final
- Celtic won the European Cup and reached another final. They also reached the European Cup Winners Cup semi-final.

Not bad eh? And who was watching? Well a lot of people. In their title-winning season, Dundee averaged close to 40,000 a game and took 20,000 to Perth to see the title won. And our own club? Here are a few snapshots: in 1962 there were 41,350 fans at Pittodrie to see a cup tie, and the following year 39,750 saw a league game between Aberdeen and the Teddy Bears. In 1965, a league match at Easter Road saw 44,300 fans crowd to Leith. And did the quality on the pitch, the huge crowds and the spread of talent show itself on the pitch? Well, between 1955 and 1966 the Scottish league had six different clubs winning the league title. Something was working. The competition drew fans who in turn increased competition; a virtuous cycle. But as in music, fashion, politics and attitudes to female nudity, the '60s did stop swinging. In 1973, 122,714 saw the Centenary Cup Final... the UK's 94th and last 100,000 football crowd. It wasn't just us... it wasn't just Scotland... something was changing. It is this change that matters.

Alan Davies, age 41, team-leader

CLUB *Aberdeen FC.*

SEASON TICKET *No.*

FIRST GAME

Cup semi-final late 1970s.

BEST MEMORY

Winning the Scottish Cup at Hampden, 1990.

WORST MEMORY

Losing to Rangers in the last game of 1990/91 season.

BEST FOOTBALL QUOTE

Have always enjoyed a non-PC shout from the crowd.

IS THE BAW BURST?

No.

How will the situation at Rangers affect Aberdeen Football Club?
Aberdeen FC will be fine, the fans have rallied behind the club and I fully expect the attendances to be up from last season and even more so if we can have a successful league campaign of challenging for 2nd, 3rd or 4th position.

How will the situation at Rangers affect Scottish football?
It is going to have mainly a positive effect, grounds will be full when Rangers visit and TV exposure will give clubs their chance to shine nationally.

It is only when Rangers reach the SPL that there may be a reaction from their fans as to perceived wrongs from the current SPL clubs and a chance to exact revenge by boycotts of away grounds. I expect that there will be a lot of animosity at several SPL grounds which will certainly spice up the atmosphere.

Scottish football needs a strong Aberdeen, why have they struggled so much in recent years?
Aberdeen have struggled so badly for years due to trying to compete with Rangers (money wise) in the early to mid '90s and also the building of the Richard Donald Stand which left the club with a hefty debt.

A string of poor managerial appointments and buying in sub-standard foreign players hasn't helped the club and it certainly lost its way in the late '90s which led to Aberdeen easily losing around 2,000 hard core fans who have yet to return to Pittodrie on a full time basis. Some make an exception when we have had a big glamour tie.

The club in recent times has also been at loggerheads with supporters groups (Red Ultras/Red Army 12) who have tried at times to inject a bit of atmosphere and colour to Pittodrie, this has led to a very poor atmosphere at the games and the team on the pitch not getting the vocal backing they deserve due to problems with stewards on the terracing.

What do we need to do to improve Scottish football?

The seven SFA performance schools is hopefully a good start, Mark Wotte must be left alone to implement all his plans.

From what I've read online on various fans forums, this seasons Under-20 league has been met with an extremely positive response; it seems the football on show has been far better than the football being played in the SPL.

Other comments

TV is a massive killer on attendances and atmosphere at matches, lunchtime kick-offs are dreaded by all fans and I myself have maybe attended three or four live SPL games over the course of the last ten years or so, as I, like many, just point blank refuse to go to a game at lunchtime on a Saturday or Sunday.

I would like to see the resurrection of SPL TV which would include the SFL leagues and play these games at a more suitable time even if it means going up against the overhyped Sky produced EPL.

7

ANNAN V RANGERS

Super Annan Welcomes Super Ally

GAME 7 FOLLOWED hot on the heels of the first two international matches of the 2014 World Cup qualifying campaign. Hopefully the disappointment of the two dismal draws would disappear over the weekend down on the Solway Firth. We were on tour again as a family and I was looking forward to returning to Annan and having the Monday off. This would probably be the last holiday before Christmas and I wanted to enjoy it. Unfortunately, it didn't get off to the best of starts and, for once, the wife wasn't to blame! A couple of hours after leaving Prestwick we found ourselves in a golf club car park. If we had followed the directions issued by the normally reliable sat-nav, we would probably still be reversing back down the dirt track just before the aforementioned club. Thankfully, we managed to turn and eventually found the caravan site a few miles down the road. The weekend started at about 8pm.

It had been another busy football week, dominated initially by the fallout from Scotland's two unremarkable home games against Serbia and Macedonia. The campaign was as good as over before it had properly begun. Many had expected a minimum of four points from the two games. Others had stated that only two wins would suffice. It was a tough group, everyone agreed on this, and I had my doubts about qualification long before the opening match. But it was a fresh start and the usual excitement and expectation preceded the game. Or so I thought. The games and the atmosphere at Hampden were subdued. The usual spring in the step of the marching Tartan Army was missing. Attendances were well down on what we would normally expect at the beginning of the journey to major tournaments at the national stadium. Something wasn't right.

After the Serbia game, I noticed some resentment towards Scotland manger Craig Levein. More worryingly, the proposed boycotts had materialised. People were disillusioned with the SFA and had voted with their feet. The Rangers situation had impacted on our national team's efforts to make our first major finals since France 1998. The deep divisions that I had highlighted during the 2010/11 review had deepened further. Would this downward spiral ever end?

Towards the end of the week, Rangers' new chief executive, Charles Green, dominated the headlines. An SPL commission was set up to look into the use of Employee Benefit Trusts (EBTs, also known as dual contracts, are a form of tax avoidance) during David Murray's reign at Ibrox. The new regime, The Rangers Football Club, would not be attending the hearings and would robustly defend the trophies and titles that had been won previously. Clearly, the new beginning is still inextricably linked with the old regime. The repercussions will no doubt continue unabated and the wounds that Rangers and Scottish football have suffered will take a long time to heal.

Normally, it's a great feeling to wake up on a Saturday. But when you're on holiday it's even better and then, when you realise that you're off to the football, hospitality et al, it's heaven! The morning was a bit rushed though, and before I knew it we were stuck in traffic in Annan. The good people of this quaint fishing port had probably seen nothing quite like the light blue invasion that had engulfed their town. The Gers fans were everywhere. Many of them were actually locals and everyone was keen to play a part in this historic day. The better half dropped me off just across from Galabank at 12.35pm, five minutes late, with instructions to return after the match – beer time!

I walked around the club house and straight into one of the main lounges. Surprisingly, none of the stewards challenged me. One chap did ask if I had any spare tickets but that was it. A good suit opens many doors! I eventually located and squeezed into my seat. They were really making the most of the space, but that was understandable and once you settled in it wasn't a problem. Everybody in close proximity introduced themselves, and that made for a warm and friendly atmosphere. The early kick-off (St Johnstone v Celtic) was on the big TVs but most people were focusing on socialising rather than the televised game. Initially, I frequently glanced at the screen but I soon lost interest because it had no relevance to my team or indeed the Third Division. I did however, look up when the biggest cheer of the day heralded the Saints winning goal.

Galabank bursting at the seams.

The food and drink was served promptly and the chatter was incessant until the chairman entered and silenced the happy crowd. He made an emotional speech that focused on today's game; the biggest in the club's history. It was rousing stuff and he got loud applause. He went on to explain about the efforts that went into readying the club for the visit of Rangers. Hours of hard graft by volunteers and a lot of money spent on upgrading the stadium. A new artificial pitch had been laid (great news for both the club and the community) and various other improvements had been undertaken. The vice-chairman, who underlined the safety rules and agenda for the rest of the day's hospitality, followed him. All very professional but with a personal touch – I was thoroughly impressed. Time for the action.

We walked out en masse and were handed stand tickets at the gate. The wee place was packed which I thought was brilliant – what a difference from my last visit. The referee got the formalities over and done with, and after the Rangers coaching staff worked out which dugout they were in, the game kicked off. You would be forgiven for thinking that the outcome of this game was a foregone conclusion. How on earth could a team that only joined the Scottish League from the East of Scotland League in 2008 compete with a team that played in the UEFA Cup Final (that very year) and regularly competed in the Champions League? The mind boggles as to how we've got to this situation!

But all credit to Annan. This wee club had arrived and they probably should have beaten Rangers. Their illustrious visitors were out of sorts. Annan never let them get into their stride and kept hounding, pressing and, more importantly, believing that they could get a result. Like the previous away matches that I'd attended, this was a good contest. The gulf that many think exists between the top and lower leagues simply isn't there when it comes to one-off matches. Yes, there is gap in quality, particularly at the lower end of the Third Division, but in situations like this the games are never going to be easy.

The first half was fast and furious. Tackles were flying in right, left and centre. The crowd was upbeat and made plenty of noise throughout. Unfortunately, the Rangers fans had seen it all before and were starting to get a bit agitated – why can't we put on a decent performance on the road?

The second half was much the same as the first. Annan probably had the better chance to claim the points but a draw was a fair result. The final whistle signaled the end of the match and we slowly returned to the clubhouse for a small buffet and another couple of complimentary drinks. The ladies that were beside me earlier also returned and were keen to reveal who was Man of the Match! I had enquired earlier about the criteria for winning. 'Simple,' was the reply, 'best looking, best legs.' They had chosen a young Annan player who had had a great game. The vice-chairman's wife, Irene, presented the prize to the bewildered youngster whom I later found out had a dual contract – he was an apprentice plumber (EBT Annan style!).

Just after returning to her seat across from me, Irene gasped and covered her face. I wondered what was going on. Then a chap leaned over my shoulder to shake her hand. The one and only Ally McCoist introduced himself. The place erupted into the famous 'Super Ally' chant. The man himself seemed a touch embarrassed and headed for the exit. Irene said she would never wash her hand again!

A text message alerted me to the fact that the wife was outside. I let her know I'd be five minutes, grabbed another pint and headed for vice-chairman Philip Jones. We were soon in deep conversation about football, and in particular community-based business models. We agreed on the benefits and I also asked if they could do a Ross

County. 'Yes', was the reply, 'but we won't get into debt in attempting to do it!' I sensed that this was a club that was developing in the proper manner. Another text message – time to go! I said my goodbyes and made for the exit. En route, Billy Sim, ex-QoS player and Annan manager, grabbed me. We chatted for another few minutes on what had been a remarkable day for the club. I've no doubt I could have stayed all night and talked football but it really was time to go.

Within minutes, I was in the big chippy ordering the wife's fish supper.

All in all, it had been a great day and I'm sure a long and great night for many of the locals. Sunday was spent (indoors – weather terrible) reflecting on the difference between my two visits to Galabank. Albion Rovers were the opposition on my last visit and contributed to a super game of football. However, the key difference is the supporters. Getting them in their thousands transforms the place and even though the game wasn't up to much, everyone will remember the first time the Rangers came to Annan.

Next up, it was the table-topping Doonhamers at Ibrox. Would there be a cup shock on the cards? Could Third Division Rangers beat the Second Division pace setters? Interesting! Anyway, enough about football, it was the wife's birthday and we had booked the spa cabin for a couple of hours. And it was fabulous – can't wait to come back to Annan again, that's what football's all about.

Quotes of the day – *'I'll never wash that hand again'* and *'Simple – best looking, best legs.'*

GAME	ANNAN ATHLETIC VERSUS RANGERS
COMPETITION	SFL3
DATE	SATURDAY 15 SEPTEMBER 2012, KO 3PM
VENUE	GALABANK
ATTENDANCE	2,517
SCORE	0-0

Some Views from the Fans

Roddy O'Hara, age 56, accountant

CLUB   *Annan Athletic* FC.

SEASON TICKET   *Yes.*

FIRST GAME

I vaguely remember going to watch a Scotland under-15 match at Palmerston.

BEST MEMORY

1973, Scotland beating Czechoslovakia 2-1 on a wild, rainy, windswept night to qualify for the 1974 World Cup.

WORST MEMORY

1990 World Cup Genoa – losing to Costa Rica.

BEST FOOTBALL QUOTE

'It's only 11 men against 11.'

IS THE BAW BURST?

No.

How will the situation at Rangers affect Annan Athletic Football Club?
Like all Third Division teams, the profile and publicity has been increased massively, not just for the club, but for the town. The players have a once in a lifetime chance to experience playing competitively against a world famous club (let's forget all the summer shenanigans). The fans have the opportunity to experience a big match atmosphere right on their own doorstep. The club has to grasp the opportunity and sharpen their focus on ensuring the stadium can cope, that people enjoy it and want to come back and also that it encourages locals to support their local team.

How will the situation at Rangers affect Scottish football?
It is a big wake-up call for everyone to manage their own affairs sensibly and not be over dependent on the big two. Rangers have taken on the new challenge with gusto, their fans are loving it – they have fallen in love with the game again. There is no bitterness in the Third Division or apathetic shows on the park. The guys may not be as skillful but give their all. As they will, no doubt remerge, lesser teams will gain some economic

advantage on the journey. The bigger teams need to get their own houses in order.

What does the future hold for AA and could they ever do a Ross County?
Annan have made tremendous advances. Ross County are unbelievable and something to aim for. Annan are first and foremost a community club – there are plans ahead to integrate community use through maximising any future facilities by encompassing all sorts of bodies, for example we need new changing rooms, (these could also be used when hiring out our pitch) hospitality rooms which could be used as meeting rooms or training rooms for all sorts of groups or organisations – from rehabilitating prisoners to salsa classes to training courses. The club has to be inclusive and something for the community to be proud of. Dumfries & Galloway is quite a low wage economy, once Chapelcross and the MOD depots close down, unless new jobs arrive this may hinder the town to prosper and as a consequence restrain the ambitions of the club.

What do we need to do to improve Scottish football?
Selfishness and self-preservation rather than the good of the game have caused many of the current problems. Forget all the scaremongering by the tabloids and the two heid men at the SPL and SFA, football will never die in Scotland – there is too much passion for it. Yes, there is plenty wrong with it – in a lot of cases for instance it is vastly overpriced. They need to listen to their customers and make it an enjoyable experience for them. Clubs need to be part of the community – never mind Ross County – Barcelona are not just a football club, they are a sports club with many other sports. Nothing like aiming high! Common sense should prevail.

Other comments
Football is entwined in all aspects of life – the positive effect it can have should be harnessed to channel energies to a better quality of life for everyone.

Craig Maclean, age 38, self-employed

CLUB   *Ross County.*

SEASON TICKET   *No.*

FIRST GAME

Goes back to the Highland League days!

BEST MEMORY

Winning the First Division 2012, beating Celtic 2-0 at Hampden to reach the Scottish Cup Final and slaughtering ICT 5-1 in their own backyard!

WORST MEMORY

Losing to ICT at end of season 2010 which meant our league hopes ended and they went on to win the First Division.

BEST FOOTBALL QUOTE

Derek Adams on the mic at Victoria Park in April 2012: 'We are the champions!'

IS THE BAW BURST?

Certainly not – it's never been a better time to follow Ross County!

How will the situation at Rangers affect Ross County Football Club?
I don't feel the Rangers situation affects Ross County at all to be honest. It's our first season in the SPL and we will sell out the games against Celtic and ICT every time and have high attendances at all our home games! It's the honeymoon period for our club and a new era which we are enjoying to the full! For the Highlands to have a local derby in the SPL is a dream scenario and something of a fairy story – it was only in the mid 1990s that we were both small Third Division sides. So Highland football is buzzing and I feel this means more than playing Rangers.

How will the situation at Rangers affect Scottish football?
Scottish football is most affected by Rangers' fierce rivals Celtic and their own fans! The situation at Rangers most affects Celtic as they won't be pushed competitively on the park and will miss the money associated with Old Firm matches. However, the fact they reached the Champions League will compensate financially. I think it's a good thing for the Third Division sides to be earning money selling out their home games to Rangers and this will continue at other clubs as they move up through the leagues. The

Rangers fans are clearly affected playing against lower league opposition and it will take them at least a decade or more to get to the level they were at previously! For Third Division players to be playing at Ibrox live on TV is something of a fairy story and I think this is a real positive from the entire situation!

Ross County have gone from the Highland League to Hampden and on into the SPL. What can other clubs learn from this journey and is it possible for other 'smaller' provincial clubs to do likewise?
If Ross County can do it, others can do it! Our story is a fairy story and a dream I never dared think we'd ever realise. To be playing in the SPL every week is incredible and a tribute to the management and players who worked hard over the years! Other clubs can learn from paying wages at a reasonable level and building a 'team ethos' amongst the players. Also, the training facilities at Ross County are in the top three in Scotland which also helps greatly attracting players north. If a small team from Dingwall can get to the SPL, anyone else can with the correct management and squad of players!

Motherwell, St Johnstone, Hearts and Dundee United have all been eliminated from Europe in their first round of matches. How can we improve on this dismal annual statistic?
I'd say we need to blood more youngsters earlier to improve Scottish football. This will take time, but with no Rangers in the SPL this may actually help as more teams will develop youngsters and throw them into the team earlier than normal. At the moment, ordinary teams from abroad are putting our ordinary Scottish teams out which is concerning. Apart from that I don't know the solutions!

What do we need to do to improve Scottish football?
Blood more youngsters and build 'team ethos' rather than pay highly paid players astromical wages to play alongside these youngsters. Wages should be fair and reflect team playing!

Other comments
Promote the positives in football. The SPL is still exciting with new teams and new venues to play at. No Highland team was in the Scottish League in April 1994. Now we have two SPL sides from the Highlands plus two in the Third Division and football up here is buzzing!

8

RANGERS V QUEEN OF THE SOUTH

Squeaky Bum Time

I WAS PARKED at 6pm in my usual spot on Urrdale Road. Kick-off wasn't until 7.45pm so I decided to write up my Annan notes for an hour before grabbing a quick pint in the Swallow Hotel. Radio Scotland was on in the background and I couldn't help noticing the lack of coverage for the night's Rangers v QoS game. The sports bulletins were dominated by Champions League news and the outcry regarding the shocking cover-ups that went on after the Hillsborough tragedy in 1989. Sir Alex Ferguson was also waxing lyrical about the sickening chants that emanate from the stands and terraces. I do agree with him. So much of it is absolute rubbish. You should just ignore it but it does get to you sometimes. Football supporters need to raise standards as well, it's not just about the clubs and the authorities.

The hour flew by and I was soon legging it over the motorway bridge towards the hotel. The bar was quiet and I was served almost immediately. I took a stool at the window and thought about the game. It's hard to believe, but I was actually worried about the night's opposition – squeaky bum time (a favourite phrase of the aforementioned Sir Alex, used at the end of the season when the title race is reaching its conclusion) right enough! The performance on Saturday was way below par and here we were facing the Second Division's form side. Incredibly, the Ramsdens Cup was suddenly a major tournament for the Gers. This is the one cup competition that we would be favourites to win. None of the big SPL clubs were in it and I'm sure it would be high on the priority list for the Ibrox management team (this was confirmed in the match programme). I finished my pint and headed for the stadium.

Dinner would be the £5 meal deal, steak pie, Bovril and crisps. Not the healthiest of options but even at Ibrox the choice remains limited. And at this point I must confess. I had been on a training course at the Inchyra Grange Hotel in Falkirk during the day. Guess what was on the lunchtime menu? Mini steak pies – I'll turn into one these things one day! I finished my food and headed out into the arena. There was a good crowd inside for a midweek fixture. In fact, QoS had the biggest travelling support I've seen at Ibrox outside an Old Firm match – great stuff. Hopefully the match would live up to expectations.

First up were the Hillsborough tributes. A flag adorned with the crests of Rangers and Liverpool was carried out to the centre circle. This was followed by an impeccably observed minute's silence. I've no doubt that many in the crowd were thinking not only of the Hillsborough victims but of the supporters who lost their lives in this very stadium. Ibrox today stands as a memorial to those who died in the 1902 and 1971 disasters. Football stadiums should be safe places with good facilities, that is a given. Too many around the country are still way below a reasonable standard and this worries me, particularly with Rangers bringing large numbers of supporters. Would some of the smaller grounds cope if something unusual happened? Hopefully the smaller clubs have thoroughly assessed the situations.

The match eventually got underway and Queens had the best chances of the opening spell. Once again, Rangers seemed lacklustre and the home crowd was nervous. The groans and jeers continued until the referee blew for half-time. The entertainment lifted the spirits during the break. The crossbar challenge grabs the attention, especially when the prize is one million pounds. Unfortunately, none of the contestants ever get near it. Most don't even reach the penalty box from their starting point at the halfway line. On current form, most Rangers players would also struggle.

Hopefully, in the second half we would see an improvement. And we did. After just four minutes, the Doonhamers deservedly took the lead. What was going on? Rangers responded and a few minutes later the game was level again. But there was still a spark missing from the host's play and things worsened just after an hour when substitute Kevin Kyle, who had only been on for ten minutes, was dismissed for his second bookable offence. Things were looking grim for the fallen giants until a penalty breathed new life into their challenge. Captain Lee McCulloch slotted away the spot-kick and all the ten men had to do now was hold out for another 15 minutes. Large swathes of the home support were heading for exits as the game reached its conclusion. But all credit to Queens. They had other ideas and kept pressing and pressing and, with almost the last kick of the ball in regulation time, they equalised. Unbelievable! We then realised that extra time beckoned. This was going to be a long hard season.

The referee had evened things up by dismissing a Queens player so the extra time period would begin with ten-a-side. The dramatic equaliser had knocked the stuffing from the Glasgow giants and they couldn't get the breakthrough that the home supporters craved. The Doonhamers held out for the additional 30 minutes and that meant a penalty shoot-out!

Unbelievable is the only way to describe the night's events. Two sent off, last second equaliser and then penalties – you couldn't make this stuff up. After a few coin tosses, the goalkeepers headed for the Broomloan end of the ground. I was pleased as this end housed the noisy Blue Order supporters and the substantial Queens following. The stadium stood in anticipation. Rangers captain McCulloch put the hosts ahead with the first spot kick. Then Lyle hit the cross bar and suddenly the Gers were in the driving seat. But not for long. Queens keeper Robinson saved from Shiels and it was game on. The next five kicks hit the back of the net. With the competition level at 3-3, Rangers' Argyriou hit the post. Up stepped McGuffie and he slotted home the winner for the Dumfries side, putting Rangers out of the Ramsdens Cup.

The Doonhamers faithful were overjoyed, and rightly so. They had beaten the once mighty Rangers on their own patch. The home support was stunned. Another hammer blow on the fragile road to recovery. I walked to the car. My worst fears from earlier had been realised. What else could go wrong? It was nearly 11.30pm when I got home. A good day had been ruined by that last second equaliser. But that's football. What's important is how you respond. I suppose the Rangers fans, myself included, felt we were due a break after everything that's gone on at the club. The new start had screeched to a halt.

It was now blatantly obvious that the early season talk of quadruples (league, Ramsdens Cup, League Cup and Scottish Cup) was way off the mark. The financial muscle of the Ibrox side off the park would need to be matched on the park. Every team that plays against them is desperate to do well and will do everything they can to get a result. The players in light blue must up the ante in every game to be sure of successfully progressing through the divisions. Anything less will result in failure.

Quote of the day? *Rangers fan – 'Extra time, they should be daeing time fur taking money under false pretences!'*

GAME	RANGERS VERSUS QUEEN OF THE SOUTH
COMPETITION	RC QF
DATE	TUESDAY 18 SEPTEMBER 2012, KO 7.45PM
VENUE	IBROX STADIUM
ATTENDANCE	23,932
SCORE	2-2 (QOS WON 4-3 ON PENALTIES)

Some Views from the Fans

David Gow, age 55, healthcare scientist.

CLUB   *Queen of the South.*

SEASON TICKET   *No.*

FIRST GAME

Queen of the South v Hamilton, 19/10/1968.

BEST MEMORY

Beating Rangers at Ibrox, September 2012.

WORST MEMORY

Challenge cup final v Ross County 2011.

BEST FOOTBALL QUOTE

'The trouble wi you son is yer brains are a' in yer heid.'

IS THE BAW BURST?

No, just a wee bit soft.

How will the situation at Rangers affect QoS Football Club?
It has caused factions already since the board voted for the newco into Division One when a significant number of fans were clearly against it. The board has subsequently tried to assert that there was a silent majority for this decision. In larger terms, competing with Rangers on an even playing field has already benefitted Queens via the win at Ibrox. In years to come we should have some good pay days when the Rangers get to the same league. Probably in a wider sense Scottish football now has to reorganise or die since no club is immune.

How will the situation at Rangers affect Scottish football?
What it does show for Scottish football is that the governance of a club cannot be a secret and that the fans need more say, albeit with sound business practices to ensure we don't let our hearts rule our heads. In short, if it can happen to Rangers…

QoS played the New Rangers at Ibrox recently. Describe the significance of this event.
For me personally, huge. The drama of the event of course contributed to that but the fact that my wee team was at one of the biggest clubs in the world and beat them on their home ground was seismic. It suggests that the gap between clubs in Scotland is not as large as some believe.

Ross County went from the Highland League to Hampden and then onto the SPL. QoS have also made it to Hampden recently – is making the SPL a possibility bearing in mind that Dumfries has almost ten times the population of Dingwall?
Yes it is, and although the precedent isn't good, Gretna showed it could be accomplished. If a similar sugar daddy had invested in Queens with a healthy fan base and more potential than Gretna, then Queens would not only have emulated Gretna but could have survived. I would, though, state that given recent events I'm not sure we want to get into the current SPL! I think we'd rather be in a competitive top tier which is larger than 12 clubs and is not a closed shop.

What do we need to do to improve Scottish football?
Sort out the so-called governing bodies. The men in blazers from the SFA, League and Junior SFA are a nonsense. We also need a pyramid system and standards for clubs/grounds and I don't mean arbitrary ones like 6,000 seats. I mean working toilets with soap and water, in stadia that have more than just football to attract kids and families.

Other comments
We need to improve the democracy of club boards. I know these are businesses but some of them are a) very small businesses and b) all of them mean a great deal more to their fans and communities than any business I've ever encountered. Every club should have to have a supporters' director (elected from a fans trust). If not, they should not be licensed to participate in Scottish football.

Richard Cook, age 53, project Support Manager

CLUB   *Raith Rovers.*

SEASON TICKET   *Yes.*

FIRST GAME

Raith Rovers v Rangers 1968 at Starks Park – lost 3-2.

BEST MEMORY

27 November 1994, League Cup Final v Celtic!

WORST MEMORY

Relegation from SPL in 1996–97.

BEST FOOTBALL QUOTE

'Three-nil up with five mins to play. Least the draw is safe.'

IS THE BAW BURST?

No.

How will the situation at Rangers affect Raith Rovers Football Club?
Don't think it will until they end up in the same league – possibly two seasons away. Their influence to get TV coverage will – as is the case in the Third Division – help the clubs financially but for the fans we can expect weird kick-off times!

How will the situation at Rangers affect Scottish football?
In the short term, SPL clubs may struggle but the lower clubs can benefit from this too. It might actually be the saving of some small clubs!

Raith Rovers had a very successful period in the nineties. Can that be re-peated and what would be required?
A miracle! No, seriously over the next few seasons the gulf between SPL clubs and the First Division will narrow, Raith will be in the top league again.

What do we need to do to improve Scottish football?
Reduce the number of foreign players and stop relying so much on TV money.

9

RANGERS V MONTROSE

Happy Birthday

ANOTHER SUNDAY KICK-OFF at Ibrox, but this time it was at 3pm which was bearable – just! I decided to leave later than normal so as to get some things done at home. This would mean parking further away from the stadium but I couldn't afford to waste time hanging about outside or whatever so I would take my chances. I ended up much further away than I anticipated and this would possibly mean heavy traffic later on. Why couldn't they just make it a Saturday so I could get the train and a couple of pints afterwards? The English premiership was also very tasty looking this afternoon. Manchester City were hosting Arsenal and Liverpool were entertaining Manchester United, but it was SFL3 for me!

Montrose were the day's visitors and a massive improvement would be required to get over being knocked out of the Ramsdens Cup. Yes, we were out of the Ramsdens – bizarre! The previous Tuesday's defeat by Queen of the South was still fresh in the memory, and the prospect of facing table topping Motherwell at Ibrox midweek had become very daunting. A good result against Montrose was essential to give the lads some confidence for the League Cup tie against the Steelmen. I headed into the stadium full of hope – as usual.

The old place was still filling up as I turned my attention to the programme. Today's Ready was a 50th birthday tribute to Super Ally. Yes, the Rangers manager would be blowing out half a century's worth of candles on Monday. So many good times and memories for the club's leading scorer over the years. His time as assistant to Walter Smith was also very successful. Supporter, player and manager, he's lived the dream. And we all know that Ally likes a bet. But never in his wild-

A quiet Sunday!

est dreams would he have bet on becoming the manager of a Rangers side plying their trade in Division Three – incredible! Happy Birthday Super Ally.

The game kicked off in front of an astonishing 45,081 crowd (more than Liverpool v Man Utd, but 2,000 short of Man City v Arsenal). Pretty quiet at the outset though, both on and off the park, and it remained so for the opening period. Montrose had the smallest number of fans I'd seen in a while and this was surprising given the significance of the day and the fact that it was a scorcher. Maybe they had decided to watch the English games on TV. Rangers opened the scoring halfway through the first half and to be honest, I expected a goal rush (again!). It never materialised, although I suppose you could count Argyriou's own goal! I was again surprised at how 'understanding' the home support was of the lacklustre performance. In years gone by, the players would have been hounded off at the interval. Instead, there were merely a few boos and shouts of discontent – changed days indeed.

I returned to the programme during the break. The week's news had again featured the Employee Benefit Trust enquiry and the seemingly never-ending pursuit of the club in any way, shape or form. There was talk of stripping titles and cup successes and even top judge Lord Nimmo Smith was compelled to explain his involvement in the latest tribunal process. When would it all end for heavens sake? Interestingly, the BBC published a (very short) piece on European regional leagues. Rangers is still part of the group, along with Aberdeen, Celtic and Hearts, and it was reported that they will attend a meeting to discuss the European idea and amongst other things – reconstruction! The story concluded that after a summer of discontent in Scottish football, there is a feeling that radical change is needed to fix the game and move it forward. I won't hold my breath!

The second half started at a much higher tempo than the first, don't know what was in the player's tea during the break but something sparked them into life. With less than ten minutes gone, Rangers had taken the lead and increased it further just on the hour. Things were clicking for the home side, and unfortunately the Gable Endies had no response. Gers youngster Fraser Aird had made a real impact and was causing the visitors all sorts of problems. A fourth goal for the home side was nothing more than they deserved, but it's worth noting that Montrose never rolled over and accepted defeat. They kept trying to the death and would be pleased with their contribution to a fabulous second half. Three points in the bag – roll on Tuesday and the SPL leaders!

Quote of the day – *Rangers fan watching the big TV: 'That premiership's a lot of pish.' Yes, bring on Montrose, I say.*

GAME	RANGERS VERSUS MONTROSE
COMPETITION	SFL3
DATE	SUNDAY 23 SEPTEMBER 2012, 3PM
VENUE	IBROX STADIUM
ATTENDANCE	45,081
SCORE	4-1

Some Views from the Fans

Robert McDougall, age 43, civil engineer

CLUB *Aberdeen (although it's really Scotland!).*

SEASON TICKET *Aberdeen – No, Scotland – Yes.*

FIRST GAME

Aberdeen 3 Hearts 0 – Scottish Cup Final 1986; Scotland 1 Peru 1 – Friendly at Hampden, 1979.

BEST MEMORY

Aberdeen – got to be Gothenburg. Scotland – the feeling walking out of Hampden having beaten Holland 1-0 in the play-offs.

WORST MEMORY

Aberdeen – Hateley scoring twice at Ibrox to deny us the league in 1991 last game of the season. We only needed a point. Was he on a dual contract?

Scotland – too many, possibly 0-6 in Amsterdam the Wednesday after beating them on the Saturday.

BEST FOOTBALL QUOTE

From my Uncle Bobby – 'Always play football on your knees. You'll look like a tit, but not half as much of a tit as you do when you get nutmegged.'

IS THE BAW BURST?

Nearly, but not quite.

How will the situation at Rangers affect Aberdeen Football Club?
Aberdeen now has a better chance of finishing second, but the club faces a possible loss of income in coming seasons should Rangers not get back in the SPL soon.

How will the situation at Rangers affect Scottish football?
There is a risk of loss of income to top flight clubs, but increased income to lower league teams as they make their way back. This might result in a

correction to top flight club finances which would get them back playing within their means, but could also result in clubs going bust.

The European co-efficient could be damaged further by poorer teams playing in Europe, but we've not been competitive for years anyway.

Scottish football needs a strong Aberdeen. Why have they struggled so much in recent years?

Because unlike Rangers, Hearts, Dundee, Motherwell, Gretna, Livingston and others, Aberdeen has tried to live within its means. We've not burst our wages limit or paid big transfer fees and so the standard of footballer we've signed has declined. We also seem to struggle to attract some players because of the geographical location, which I don't remember being an issue in years gone by.

What do we need to do to improve Scottish football?

Financial fair play or wages limits or franchises. Not just in Scottish football, but worldwide. FIFA and UEFA have ruined the game internationally and in Europe chasing the big bucks and paying it to the top clubs and the FA has done likewise in England (best league in the world? Only four teams have won it since 1995!) Spain is just as bad if not worse. Spanish club supporters outwith the top two recently had a protest where they sported banners stating 'We don't want another Scottish League'. FIFA and UEFA need to be told that their responsibility is to all member associations and clubs, not just the elite.

We need something like a franchise model where players' contracts are owned and paid for by the governing body. At least then we'd have some parity and someone else would have a chance of winning. We also need nationality quotas again to stop the foreign dross coming to Scotland and choking development of young talent (surely we've got better Scottish strikers than Sandaza, Higdon, Fallon, Doyle?)

Gate and catering prices must come down. It shouldn't cost the best part of £100 for me to take my lad to a top flight football match. I'd expect hospitality for that!

Here's one from left of centre: get rid of transfer fees. Club finances would be more regular and consistent and not dependent on cashing in on lucky finds. Youth development would be about producing better players for the sake of it instead of to make money out of them.

The next big thing Scotland needs to do is get rid of the Old Firm. All they do is bring bigotry and misery, and they're both far too big for the rest now anyway. Let them go to England, start at the bottom, and within four to six years they'll both be in the Premier League where they want to be. With the current situation, nobody else will win the league in my lifetime and that's sad. My Hearts supporting, football daft nephew is 27 and he can't remember anyone else winning the league.

If we got rid of them, the league would suddenly become much more competitive. Teams like Hearts, Dundee Utd and Motherwell would have a chance of winning immediately and it wouldn't take the others long to catch up. We must do it soon, because at the moment we still have older fans who can remember it being more competitive, and they would drag along younger fans who don't currently go to games or only go occasionally. Within a couple of years, the teams challenging for the league would have full houses again and within five to ten years it will have filtered through all of the top flight clubs.

Failing getting rid of the Old Firm, move to a 16 team top league. Play each other twice, home and away, then split into top 4, middle 8 and bottom four. Top four play semis and final to decide the league (Old Firm would LOVE that – not!). Middle 8 play quarters, semis and final for a trophy. Bottom team relegated, top of Division One promoted. Next three bottom clubs join with second place Division One and play semis and final to decide remaining place. Everybody's got something to play for till almost the end of the season, with all finals played at Hampden, or suitable sized neutral ground.

I HAVE A DREAM!

Other comments

The loss of income to top flight clubs doesn't particularly bother me. All clubs need to start living within their means and shouldn't be reliant on any other club to do so. Any club, including Aberdeen, who can't do this should fold and start again, just like Rangers in Division Three, or lower if necessary.

Enjoyed the first book immensely, but we shouldn't bring back drinking at games. We've still got far too much of a social problem in Scotland with alcohol which needs to be sorted before we go down that route.

Paul Martin, age 47, company director

CLUB *None presently, formerly Albion Rovers.*

SEASON TICKET *No.*

FIRST GAME

Went to see the Accies with my dad.

BEST MEMORY

Beating Airdrie 7-2.

WORST MEMORY

Losing 1-0 to Sunnybank in the Scottish Cup 2010/11 season.

BEST FOOTBALL QUOTE

'Everybody will be playing 6/4 formation in years to come.'

IS THE BAW BURST?

Has been for quite a while.

How will the situation at Rangers affect Albion Rovers Football Club?
Presently the loss of Airdrie United (due to Rangers' demotion) will cost
the Rovers 20k plus in loss of revenue stream. The promotion of Stranraer
also means that costs for the season will rise.

How will the situation at Rangers affect Scottish football?
A lot of interest in the bottom division (live matches at Peterhead!). The
sustainability of this interest is questionable. Rangers are a huge brand
and are probably a greater revenue generator than all of the SFL clubs
put together. There will undoubtably be a spin off in the lower League
Cup competitions. What odds are Rangers for the Ramsdens Cup, for
example?

What does the future hold for a club like Albion Rovers?
I believe the future for Albion Rovers is bright. An enthusiastic young
manager and a chairman who operates within their revenue stream means
that come 2013/2014 they will be a trading business.

Inverness CT and Ross County have made it to the SPL from the Highland League. What's stopping the Wee Rovers making it to the top tier of Scottish football?
The Wee Rovers will do well to secure another year in the Second Division. In fact it would be an amazing achievement to survive again. The lack of community interest restricts revenue stream at the moment but with potentially a new stadium in the plans and council support the Rovers could one day be a stable First Division club.

What do we need to do to improve Scottish football?
More support to the infrastructure of the game. More investment in community clubs. More kids playing football at their local clubs. Less focus on the Old Firm.

Other comments
An introduction of wage capping in the SFL would restrict the overspending that goes on in the game.

10

RANGERS V MOTHERWELL

Judgement Day

GAME 10 STARTED with a complaint. TV scheduling had stipulated a 7.15pm kick-off and I had a meeting in Glasgow that started at 6pm and would go on for at least 90 minutes. Why not 7.45pm as usual? Normally I wouldn't have minded the earlier start, in fact I think it makes sense, but TV rules the roost and we all need to alter our schedules to suit them. I made my apologies and left the meeting at 7pm and headed for Ibrox in a Fast Black. I'd parked over there earlier and got the subway back into town – the things we do to see the Rangers. This was one game that I didn't want to miss for a number of reasons. First and foremost, this would be a benchmark for the team and I was intrigued to discover how far we'd fallen behind or otherwise. Playing the form team and the SPL leaders would be the ultimate test of the season to date. I was worried!

I took my usual seat just after 7.30pm and was quickly brought up to speed by my neighbour. 'We're doing well so far,' he told me. I wondered if he was watching through blue-tinted glasses but he wasn't. The Gers were playing some of their best football of the season and looked every bit an SPL side. I was pleasantly surprised, particularly when considering last week's defeat to QoS and our dreadful away form.

The home side was dictating the play and did so for the majority of the opening period. This was another act of defiance. The injustice of the summer's debacle was being redressed on the football pitch and unfortunately Motherwell were the victims. I say unfortunately because by all accounts the Lanarkshire club were willing to help the beleaguered Glasgow side on the now infamous 4 July, the day when they were expelled from the SPL. This decision will rankle with sup-

Real season tickets!

porters of Rangers for many years to come.

I was enjoying my second taste of an SPL team in action this sea-son. It's amazing the difference a few weeks makes to the teams in terms of fitness, sharpness and ultimately the tempo the game is played at. The opening day encounter at Kilmarnock when Dundee were the visitors was staid in comparison. This game was pleasing on the eye and the home side had raised their game for their illustrious visitors. The first half ended all square, and that was a fair outcome. The two teams had one good chance apiece and had two players injured. Sadly for Rangers' Sandaza, his injury was more serious but his replacement would make a significant contribution to the game. 8pm and it was half-time – at least I'd be home sharp!

Five minutes into the second half, Ibrox exploded into life. Ex-Motherwell player and Rangers captain Lee McCulloch headed the home side in front after a nice cross from Shiels. The place was bounc-ing and, for the first time in many months, bursting with expectation. The euphoria in the stands was transcending to the football pitch and Rangers got another one six minutes later. The 29,000 odd Rangers fans in the stadium were giving it big licks. The SPL, SFA and anyone else that had put the boot into the club over the last few months were on the receiving end of the verbal abuse. Super Ally was enjoying the moment and he regularly applauded the vociferous Blue Order. Some justice had been administered, and the game finished 2-0.

Myself and many others stayed long after the final whistle to applaud the teams from the park. Motherwell didn't play as well as they had been, but maybe that was down to the 'Rangers effect'. The hosts had a point to prove and they proved it with gusto. The visitors never really got going and that surprised me. Their paltry support was also a bit odd, as this was easily their best chance to beat Rangers in years. They could only have had a couple of hundred in the stadium, much less than QoS had brought the previous midweek. There had been talk of a boycott but these things are hard to judge. A midweek away game on the TV at £16 per ticket plus travel costs etc is hardly appealing. So all credit to the Gers fans for turning out in their numbers again. Ibrox reveled in the victory.

Quote of the day – *Rangers fan: 'Is that flag too heavy for you to lift linesman?'*

GAME	RANGERS VERSUS MOTHERWELL
COMPETITION	LC R3
DATE	WEDNESDAY 26 SEPTEMBER 2012, 7.15PM
VENUE	IBROX STADIUM
ATTENDANCE	29,413
SCORE	2-0

Some Views from the Fans

Neil Fox, age 23, vet

CLUB *Motherwell.*

SEASON TICKET *No.*

FIRST GAME

Hibernian (H), 1994.

BEST MEMORY

Fitzpatrick's last minute goal against Hearts in CIS semi or 'Skippy Sunday.'

WORST MEMORY

Phil O'Donnell.

BEST FOOTBALL QUOTE

'Paterson ya troglodyte.'

IS THE BAW BURST?

Temporarily deflated.

How will the situation at Rangers affect Motherwell Football Club?
In the short term we will feel the pinch financially, however, the opportunities that it has presented us with more than make up for it. I never thought I'd ever see Well play in the Champions League and I believe we have a much better chance of winning a cup this year. Long term, if we play our cards right, I believe it'll be a great thing for us.

How will the situation at Rangers affect Scottish football?
Again, finances will be adversely affected in the short term, and it's not great for our European coefficient, but then it's been ages since the Old Firm did anything in Europe anyway. The real effect depends on how the clubs react. The main focus should be on ensuring that when Rangers come back the change means there is a fairer voting system in the SPL and a more even distribution of wealth between all clubs in Scotland. There is also the positive effect of Rangers playing against lower league teams, for those teams financially, but also personally for their players it's a massive opportunity.

Motherwell FC has experienced administration, what has the club learned from that situation?

We've learned to live within our own means, and for the most part our support has learned to be happy with the fact that our club still exists and remains in the top tier of Scottish football.

Motherwell, St Johnstone, Hearts and Dundee United have all been eliminated from Europe in their first round of matches. How can we improve on this dismal annual statistic?

We need more grassroots-level coaching and to look after our youngsters better. However, unfortunately there is an attitude problem in our players caused by the society that they grow up in. Generally, in comparison to other countries, our players are lazier in their attitude to training, drink too much and there are too many of them on drugs (thankfully not too many publicly known for it at Motherwell). Unfortunately, due to a combination of factors and lack of money due to proximity to England, I can't see it changing.

What do we need to do to improve Scottish football?

We need to create a more even competition which people will want to watch, and invest in youth facilities and coaching for kids. We also need to re-invent the pathway to professional football to ensure less players slip through the net, educate young players in how to reach the top (big name foreign players to speak to them?) and how to conduct themselves and look after their bodies.

Roy Callaghan, age 47, company director

CLUB *Celtic.*

SEASON TICKET *Investors Lounge tickets.*

FIRST GAME

Clydebank V Celtic.

BEST MEMORY

UEFA Cup final.

WORST MEMORY

UEFA Cup final.

BEST FOOTBALL QUOTE

Henrik Larsson's first game when he came on for Celtic. He lost the ball to Chic Charnley to score against Celtic. The guy beside me said, 'I don't like the looks of him, he doesn't look like a player.'

IS THE BAW BURST?

Yes.

How will the situation at Rangers affect Celtic Football Club?
I felt it was right and fitting for Rangers to be demoted and enjoyed it at the time. However, I do miss the encounters and the atmosphere when Celtic play Rangers. I look forward to playing and beating Rangers in the near future once they have served their punishment. Celtic should continue to improve as a club without Rangers and hopefully improve Scottish football's standings in Europe at the same time. Celtic are managed very well from the boardroom these days and will continue to operate within their budget each year, this will maintain the future and the history of the club. Other Premier League clubs will miss Rangers more than Celtic, this will be proven in the fullness of time.

How will the situation at Rangers affect Scottish football?
I think the situation will give the lower league teams a shot in the arm. Rangers should pass through each league, possibly each year, so the smaller teams should benefit quite considerably, each team hopefully getting their moment of glory on TV and the increased revenues Rangers will bring to their door.

The 'new' Rangers are plying their trade in Division Three. Was this the right decision?
I think the punishment fits the crime at the moment. To me, they abused the system, whether that was intentional has yet to be seen, but I suspect it was. It was unbelievable when all the top stars started arriving at Ibrox back in the day, the quote 'every fiver you spend we will spend a tenner', sums it up for me. Rangers were bragging they had more money than Celtic and now we understand why. Things didn't quite fit with Scottish football at the time. They reaped the benefits of this over the years and obviously enjoyed their success. Was it fair? I don't think so, although this has yet to be proven!

What does the future hold for Celtic and Rangers, assuming Rangers make it back to the top tier of Scottish football?
When Rangers arrive back in the Premier League, things will return to the way they were, the rivalry will pick up momentum again. Both clubs will be holding on to the dream that one day they will play in the English Premiership, dominating Scottish football between them in the meantime with a taste of the Champions League thrown in.

What do we need to do to improve Scottish football?
A single organisation running Scottish football would help. Then, getting all the clubs to work together with the organisation to improve things instead of constantly fighting and withdrawing players from the national squad due to all the agendas going on. This would be a step in the right direction; if you get the basics right it's amazing what can be achieved.

11

FORRES V RANGERS

Police Station, Forres

GAME 11 OF an unbelievable season finally became a reality late on Friday afternoon. I had almost given up hope when a text message arrived confirming that the much sought after brief was mine and Forres would be the destination the following day. I must admit, the prospect wasn't at all appealing. A nine hour round trip to see Rangers struggle against another team of part-timers wasn't my favoured option on my beloved Saturday. Surely they would get it together away from home and batter a few goals in for the weary fans? Here's hoping!

I left Prestwick just after 10am and headed for Glasgow to pick up my ticket. Just over four hours later, I was in the beautiful Moray town. I was confused. The wee place looked as if it had had a makeover by the staff from the Rangers Megastore. The streets and buildings were covered in red, white and blue – quite a sight. The Gers fans had again travelled (although many were locals as well) in huge numbers and they were enjoying the atmosphere. I did a quick recce of the town and stadium and parked on Market Street.

The journey north had been uneventful. The familiar antics that characterise an away fixture for the Glasgow team do make me laugh though, and today's was a cracker. In a layby just north of Aviemore, someone had painted 'Jesus Saves' on a large rock. The stopping place had obviously been used as an unofficial toilet for the many coaches and minibuses heading to the game. One of the Bears had adorned the rock with a scarf and club crest. It was hilarious. Whether Jesus was saving Rangers or Jesus was a Rangers supporter, we could have done with some holy intervention a few months ago. I just wish I had taken a picture.

Radio Scotland was my choice of listening en route and the presenters and pundits babbled away in the background whilst I finalised my investments for the afternoon. *Off the Ball* had been talking about letting kids in free and reintroducing standing areas at top flight clubs. I definitely agree, but when is someone actually going to do something other than talk about it, is it that difficult?

On the Ball followed Stuart and Tam and I was flabbergasted by one of the statistics that they aired. Celtic's visit to Fir Park today would be their first 3pm kick-off at an away ground on a Saturday since 2005. When is this nonsense going to end? We need somebody to lead us out of the football wilderness and stand up to the forces that are ruining the game. Where are you?

A few minutes after leaving the car, I was strolling along the river across from the very busy Mosset Tavern. What a lovely setting, pity about all the police. I assumed that the stadium was simultaneously hosting the annual G8 summit. Why the need for so many police? I've yet to see any trouble whatsoever this season, maybe that's the reason why? After making my way through various cordons, I was eventually corralled into a corner and entered Mosset Park, home of the Can Cans, for the first time. And as usual, I was looking forward to the game.

The players were out on the pitch doing their warm-ups as I settled on a decent vantage point. It was quickly apparent that I would be facing another Berwick scenario with regards to viewpoints. I decided to get lunch before making a final decision and made my way to the caravan. The food available was certainly different from the normal outlets. Venison was all the rage but, me being me, I plumped for a sausage roll (edible) and a Bovril (worst ever!). I headed back towards my initial spot, taking photographs along the way. The locals who lived in close proximity to the ground were making the most of the occasion with many a party underway in the gardens and living rooms overlooking the pitch. Game on in Forres!

The game started at good tempo but unfortunately, quality football was lacking. It was hard and fast out there. Being so close to the action always emphasises the speed that the modern game is played at. Rangers broke the deadlock at 13 minutes and, yes, we expected a goal fest. But yet again, it never materialised and the teams slugged it out until half time. A poor show was further blighted by the continual taunting of Radio Clyde's Gerry McCulloch in the press area (temporary scaffold) adjacent to me. Some of the Gers faithful had

Executive box, Forres-style.

taken umbrage at his comments about attendances and had relentlessly mocked him throughout the opening period. Give it rest and watch the football.

I amused myself for a few seconds reading through the programme before heading to the toilets. The plastic boxes were functioning fairly well but had no hand washing facilities. Welcome to the lower reaches of Scottish football! As usual, a few of the Gers faithful wandered off back to the pub during the break. I was just happy to move about as the old back was playing up. Standing on a grass slope cannot be good for the posture. I longed for a seat in the stand. Terraced areas are always an option, definitely, but they're for the younger folk!

Unfortunately, it wasn't a game of two halves. Rangers never built on their lead and the second half was almost a carbon copy of the first. One exception was the sending-off of Sharp, but even against a ten-man Forres no goal fest was forthcoming for Rangers. This was definitely the quietest the travelling supporters had been this season. There was however, one rousing moment. The Forres number three (who had been getting pelters) suddenly gestured towards the Rangers support. 'We are the people', he shouted with a clenched fist. The Gers fans applauded loudly. I wondered what his manager would have thought about it, fraternising with the opponents? I was relieved when the referee ended the game. Anything was better than that performance, even a four-hour drive.

I thought long and hard about the Rangers situation all the way home. Falkirk and Brechin apart (neither were convincing), why can't they get a decent result away from home? OK, we've yet to be beaten on the road but it's imminent. The performances away from Ibrox have been unacceptable. The manager knows this but do the players? To me it's pretty simple. Keep the ball off the opposition and let them run themselves into the ground trying to get it back. Possession, possession, possession. Rangers have better players, and more of them, than the majority of teams we've played so far this season. So the obvious tactic is to keep the ball as much as possible. They should be capable of doing that.

I decided to take a break on the way home so stopped off in Auchterarder for a bag of chips. I chose the wrong chippie though. My favourite one is the first one you pass when you're heading north but I always forget and get them mixed up. I stopped at the one across from the town hall and wasn't too impressed. It broke up the journey though and I was home just over an hour later. Perfect timing for the Ryder Cup which was unfolding on TV. What a summer of sport it had been so far, incredible. And here I was, another new team and stadium visited on this latest escapade with the Gers in Division Three and playing Scottish Cup ties in September – you really couldn't make this stuff up.

Quote of the day – *Rangers fan: 'Away you go linesman and take yer* SFA *issue haircut way ye.'*

GAME	FORRES MECHANICS VERSUS RANGERS
COMPETITION	SC R2
DATE	SATURDAY 29 SEPTEMBER 2012, 3PM
VENUE	MOSSET PARK
ATTENDANCE	2,750
SCORE	0-1

Some Views from the Fans

Joe Richardson, age 53, health and safety manager

CLUB *Motherwell FC.*

SEASON TICKET *No.*

FIRST GAME

Motherwell v Partick Thistle, 1967.

BEST MEMORY

Motherwell winning the Scottish Cup in 1991.

WORST MEMORY

Being beaten 7-1 by Celtic.

BEST FOOTBALL QUOTE

'Keep the high balls low.'

IS THE BAW BURST?

Not yet.

How will the situation at Rangers affect Motherwell Football Club?
Motherwell will suffer financially and also Motherwell v Rangers at Fir Park were games to look forward to.

How will the situation at Rangers affect Scottish football?
As above, everyone will be affected plus other countries will see Scottish football being a shambles and possibly corrupt.

Motherwell FC has experienced administration. What has the club learned from that situation?
Live within your means and develop talent within the youth set-up.

Motherwell, St Johnstone, Hearts and Dundee United have all been eliminated from Europe in their first round of matches. How can we improve on this dismal annual statistic?
These teams win various domestic competitions and get into Europe, at the end of the season they generally sell players or let go players they had on loan. The European games start before or at the same time as our seasons start, the other teams are well into their seasons and we are still

cold and trying to get a settled team.

What do we need to do to improve Scottish football?
Lower the price for hiring parks, I have run boys teams for years, we cannot afford to play on astro parks when the grass parks are put off because of bad weather. More all-weather parks could be built and costs could go down.

Other comments
Better coaching, getting more people who played at a higher level to help out at youth football.

Andrew Guy, age 19, student

CLUB *Falkirk.*

SEASON TICKET *No.*

FIRST GAME

Can't remember – too young, but was at the old Brockville.

BEST MEMORY

Winning to stay in the SPL at Inverness, last day of the season 08/09.

WORST MEMORY

Relegation – every time it happens.

IS THE BAW BURST?

No.

How will the situation at Rangers affect Falkirk Football Club?
It doesn't really affect Falkirk until Rangers reach the First Division. Then Falkirk will benefit from the higher attendances, but there may be reconstruction before then.

How will the situation at Rangers affect Scottish football?
It depends on what the SPL/SFL/SFA do. If it remains as is, no-one will really benefit above SFL Division Two. It also depends how quickly Rangers are promoted. The way it's going, it won't be this season anyway!

Falkirk have previously enjoyed SPL/top league status. Do they belong in the top league and would they prosper in an extended SPL1 & 2?
As things stand, Falkirk belong in the SFL1. Falkirk would obviously benefit from an extended SPL and this would be welcomed. A 16-team league would be my preference.

What do we need to do to improve Scottish football?
16-team SPL. Getting rid of the Old Firm would result in most teams going bust due to lack of TV money and sponsorship, so the Old Firm need to stay in Scotland.

Will they ever finish the stadium?
Yes, but only if Falkirk get back into the top flight. The local council own the stadium so the problem is it's not one of their priorities.

12

STIRLING V RANGERS

Bollock!

FIRST SATURDAY AT HOME for while. I was primed and ready to go up until 1.30pm but my last chance of a ticket never materialised. I would miss out on this episode of the new Rangers' journey and would have to make do with radio and Internet updates. I was a wee bit annoyed as I had put a lot of effort in recently to get to the matches, particularly the ones that required travelling long distances. The momentum builds up as well, it becomes a habit, home and away watching your team. And another thing – this would probably be the day of the long-awaited goal fest! Anyway, not to worry, a break would do me good and with the World Cup qualifying the following week it would mean a fortnight without football. I'd had no luck with those tickets either so a chance to catch up on everything was actually quite appealing.

I eventually settled down for the afternoon and started planning the day's investments. Whilst going through the divisions I noticed that Ayr United were hosting Albion Rovers. Should I head along? I mulled over this one for an hour or so but ultimately decided to stay at home and do some work. I still shoved a few quid on Ayr though!

Three pm passed me by. I was thoroughly engrossed in my work. Reading the fans views on Scottish football was really interesting. The first thing that strikes you is their love of the game. Many of these people have been going to football all their lives. Their knowledge and passion is exemplary and they must have a say in the future of the game. My state of deep thought and consideration quickly changed to shock and humiliation. Stirling Albion were leading Rangers 1-0. What on earth was going on? The Binos are currently the worst team in Scotland. This should be 'monkey off back day.' Still, it was early enough in the game (eight minutes) for Rangers to get back into it.

The radio commentators were confident that this would be the case. I quickly checked my investments (looking good) before returning to my work.

Half-time and it was still 1-0. This was verging on the ridiculous. The Albion didn't even have their manager at the game as he was away getting married! I wondered how the Rangers fans would be reacting. They've been very supportive so far but there's only so much that they will take before they demand action. This was awful but I suppose it had been coming. We'd lost goals in most games this season, both home and away and probably more than I expected. But hold on. We've got a new team, the club is rebuilding and everybody and their granny in this division will want to beat us. What can we really expect? I think I need to tone down my aspirations a wee bit.

The automatic update on the BBC football page indicated that the game was again under way. I continued working the best I could but the live scores were a real distraction and a worry as well. Time was marching on. Text messages were coming and going. Rangers fans everywhere were worried. Would this be the worst result in our history? I tried to focus on my own investments, which were still looking good, just needed Forfar to get another one against Alloa. 4.45pm was fast approaching. Still 1-0. Damn! Alloa had just scored to make it 3-2 away to Forfar – only minutes to go as well, that was the coupon burst. The match reports were all changing to red with the letters FT displayed. It was now full-time at almost all of the grounds that had started at 3pm. Still they played at Forthbank. Could a last second equaliser save the blushes of the Glasgow giants? Eventually, yellow turned to red and FT appeared. Stirling Albion 1 Rangers 0.

Tough one to take for all Gers supporters but all credit to the Binos, they've not had their troubles to seek over the past few years. Captain Lee McCulloch described it as the most disappointing result of his Rangers career. I must admit I've felt worse after other defeats, particularly in Europe, and in hindsight it had been coming. Brechin, Peterhead, Berwick, Annan and Forres could all have gone either way. Maybe this was the wake-up call they needed. Time to roll the sleeves up and get stuck in. Time for me to get stuck into the beer in the fridge!

So a wee break now from the domestic side of things. Scotland were back in action and up against Wales on the Friday night. Hopefully the dark blues would kick-start their campaign with a win in Cardiff. Two home draws had significantly reduced my chances of being in Brazil in 2014. Why do I bother?

Quote of the day – *Radio Clyde pundit Gordon Daziel: 'If Stirling beat Rangers I'll run up and down Sauchiehall Street naked.'*

GAME	STIRLING ALBION VERSUS RANGERS
COMPETITION	SFL3
DATE	SATURDAY 6 OCTOBER 2012, 3PM
VENUE	FORTHBANK
ATTENDANCE	3,751
SCORE	1-0

Some Views from the Fans

Alasdair Mitchell, age 44, managing director

CLUB *St Mirren.*

SEASON TICKET *Yes.*

FIRST GAME

St Mirren v Clydebank in 1976.

BEST MEMORY

Winning Scottish Cup Final v Dundee Utd in 1987.

WORST MEMORY

Losing to Hammarby in the UEFA Cup 1985.

BEST FOOTBALL QUOTE

'Thank God that's the season started, maybe we can get back to watching football rather than hearing about Rangers every 5 minutes.' – Michael Clayton (my oldest and best friend) 04/08/2012.

IS THE BAW BURST?

No.

How will the situation at Rangers affect St Mirren Football Club?

St Mirren FC has been in far worse financial positions than any we will face due to the situation at Rangers and survived. We have spent the majority of the last two decades playing our football outwith the SPL while getting rid of debt from previous overspending and, as a club, are the better for it. We tend to have players on two-year or less contracts and would be able to cut our cloth if required. That aside, I don't know any fans who followed St Mirren just so that they could see St Mirren play against Rangers, or Celtic for that matter. It won't in any way change the enjoyment I get from watching my club and I'm sure that's true of most other St Mirren supporters.

How will the situation at Rangers affect Scottish football?

If we are only looking at the financial aspect then I am sure there are some clubs that will struggle should there be a reduction in income from TV and sponsors.

I think that this is an opportunity for Scottish football to pull together and move forward from the 'Old Firm duopoly' and put itself in a position where Scottish football lives within its means. If the SPL, in particular, has taught us anything it is that throwing cash at players and overspending in general does not generate success.

The Saints have a good infrastructure in place and appear to be on a sound financial footing. What does the future hold for the club and can we expect top six finishes and European football?
We have seen the club move forward in the last decade both financially and from a playing perspective. Under the current board we have progressed from second bottom of the First Division to eighth position in last year's SPL. Top six and European football would be nice but not at any cost!

Motherwell, St Johnstone, Hearts and Dundee United have all been eliminated from Europe in their first round of matches. How can we improve on this dismal annual statistic?
So not much has changed in the last three years or for much of the last ten years for that matter. Let's be honest, the 'Old Firm' have been eliminated in their first round matches in recent years too.

Creating fairer competition and spending what money we have on developing homegrown talent would be what I would like to see. Too many average players with no 'emotional' attachment to either clubs or country in our game.

What do we need to do to improve Scottish football?
Pretty much as above. We have decent coaches and decent young footballers in Scotland, we just need to create an environment in which they can flourish. We spend far too much time and energy running our game down. Scottish football needs to believe in itself and not be swamped in the apathy generated by an, all too often, agenda-led media. Good planning, hard work and self-belief would see a massive improvement!

Callum McDougall, age 19, student

CLUB   *Hibernian*

SEASON TICKET *Yes*

FIRST GAME

Hibernian v St Mirren, Div 1, season 98/99.

BEST MEMORY

Winning the League Cup March 2007, also watching the team with Brown, Thomson, Riordan and O'Connor in it. I don't think I'll see a better Hibs team in my lifetime.

WORST MEMORY

2012 Scottish Cup Final defeat to Hearts.

BEST FOOTBALL QUOTE

The guy in the West Stand who used to shout 'Steven Fletcher, you're useless!' Best player Hibs have produced in the modern era.

IS THE BAW BURST?

No – it's just the people running the game who are.

How will the situation at Rangers affect Hibernian Football Club?
Reduced revenue. Slight positive impact on Hibs chances in the league. Rangers bought Dean Shiels when he would probably have signed for Hibs. I don't think Rangers would have signed him had they been in the SPL. Transfer embargo should have been more stringently enforced, not fudged.

How will the situation at Rangers affect Scottish football?
Positive impact for lower league clubs' finances, negative effect on lower league competition. Positive effect on competition in SPL, but negative effect financially.

Hibernian FC has underachieved in recent seasons. What needs to be done to get Hibs challenging for major honours, including the league title, on a regular basis?
Proper investment – we have an owner who sold Kwik-Fit to Ford for £1billion, but won't invest in the team. He should either invest in the club or sell it. We need a Director of Football, and we need managerial stability

by putting the current manager on a long term contract. Get rid of the Old Firm from Scottish football to give others a chance to win the SPL.

Motherwell, St Johnstone, Hearts and Dundee United have all been eliminated from Europe in their first round of matches. How can we improve on this dismal annual statistic?
By bringing on our youth players and improving our game at grass roots level. Smaller, less competitive games for youth footballers. Better facilities, better coaching, copy the Spanish model.

What do we need to do to improve Scottish football?
- Get rid of the Old Firm.
- Make a 16-team SPL1, a 16-team SPL2, regional leagues below with promotion to/relegation from SPL2.
- Play offs for both divisions.
- Introduce summer football.
- Reduced/capped ticket prices.
- Nationality quotas.
- Drafting system like Major League Soccer to promote and protect Scottish youth players.

13

RANGERS V QUEEN'S PARK

Derby Day

AFTER A TWO-WEEK BREAK I was primed and ready for my 12th Rangers game of season 2012/13. I'd missed out on tickets for the two international matches in Cardiff and Brussels so I needed my football fix. The disappointment of losing in Wales and Belgium would linger for a while. For me personally, another World Cup qualifying campaign was over and it was highly unlikely that I would be going to Brazil in 2014. After only four games, we are as good as out and the Tartan Army will miss the carnival in the country that has for so long symbolised the beautiful game. The names roll off the tongue – Pelé, Rivelino, Socrates, Zico, Romario, Carlos, Ronaldinho... the list goes on and on. For Scotland, it is back to the drawing board for France 2016! And yes, it was only 20 October, 2012. Remember the good old days when we used to qualify for every World Cup and even the odd European Championship?

Today was another throwback to a bygone era, it was derby day in Glasgow. But it wasn't the usual opponents for the Gers. Yes, they still had a striped jersey but the colours were black and white rather than green and white. This was the original Glasgow derby that was first played out in 1872. The Spiders were back at Ibrox for a league match for the first time since 1958. Pity it had been so long. The boys from Hampden were instrumental in creating the game that has dominated the sporting calendar in this country ever since. It was good to welcome them back to Ibrox. Rangers versus Queen's Park had a strange but comfortable feel to it. Maybe it was time to look to the past for ideas for the future. In 1867, a number of gentlemen met for the purpose of forming a football club that went on to lay down codes, rules and regulations that many a football association across the world

The Rangers end.

adopted and use to this day. Is it time for a number of gentlemen (and ladies this time) to sit down again?

I had plenty of time to mull this over as I walked towards the Big Hoose. I was parked away over by the Sherbrooke Hotel which is a good 15 minute walk from the stadium. This indicated that a big crowd would be inside the ground which was good news for Rangers and the Spiders players who would hopefully enjoy a near capacity stadium. Their own patch at Hampden, with a 50,000 capacity, is a strange place to play in with only a few hundred supporters in the stand. I crossed over the M8 footbridge, to a chorus of horns from Celtic fans returning from their early kick-off in Paisley, and down towards Edmiston Drive and my usual programme man. No sign of any programmes, only half-time draw tickets left. Similar story at all the other outlets. The 'Original Glasgow Derby' theme had obviously captured the imagination of the supporters – memorabilia was a must.

Disappointed, I headed in and up to the snack bar for a Bovril. No pie today, watching the old weight and back in the gym a couple of times a week – still on the beer though! I took my seat but was quickly back on my feet for the 'show racism the red card' display. The majority of fans applauded the display on the pitch and after a blast of Penny Arcade (place always bounces to this one) we were underway at Ibrox.

For the first ten minutes things were bearable. After that it was a complete drag. What was going on? We were now eight games into the league season and playing at home. All due respect to our opponents, but we should have been comprehensively beating them here. This lot are amateurs for heavens sake. Rangers stuttered and misfired all through the first half. Former SPL players, some of them internationalists, just couldn't get to grips with the boys from the national stadium. Yes, the referee was a bit erratic but that probably evened itself out over the game. The pace was too slow, the ball was in the air far too often and the chances were few and far between. All in all it was a terrible first half. It reminded me of an early season game. The ref blew for half time – I really wished I had managed to get a programme!

The break seemed longer than it usually was. The cheerleaders – riveting stuff – followed the 'hit the crossbar' competition. At least the home side were out sharp. Hopefully they had had a rollicking from the manger and were raring to go. No sign of the Spiders though. Another few minutes passed before they eventually crawled out. The second half got underway and normal service was resumed. It really was a strange game. No player managed to take the game by the scruff of the neck and stamp his authority on it. It occurred to me that that had been the case so often this season both at home and away. Rangers need somebody to orchestrate the proceedings. Unfortunately, I don't think that type of player exists in the current squad. Hopefully, one will develop over the coming months. But all credit to the Queen's Park boys. They rolled up their sleeves and got stuck in and were unfortunate not to score on a couple of occasions.

Eventually the deadlock was broken. Rangers captain McCulloch slotted home after some good work from Shiels on the wing. Would this signal a goal rush? No. The Spiders hit back a few minutes later and should have been level. Mediocre was the only way to describe the remainder of the half until Barrie McKay struck a sweet 30 yarder that came off the crossbar and left McCulloch a tap in for his second of the afternoon. The last action was a clash of heads between two Gers players and after the magic sponge had done the business the ref ended the game. The Rangers players trooped off. The Queen's players headed towards their supporters to soak up the applause. I walked out into the glorious autumn sunshine.

Technically, it had been a good day at the office for the home side. They had beaten the league leaders and now topped the division. An incredible 49,463 people had watched the game, which, incidentally, was a new world record for a fourth tier game. The club had also announced that there was huge interest in the share scheme and that around £17 million had been pledged so far. Things were definitely more promising than they were a few months ago under the stewardship of Craig Whyte. The former owner had been interviewed during the week. To say my blood was boiling as I listened was the understatement of the century. How can anyone be fooled by this guy? David Murray, what were you thinking about? Anyway, we are where we are and we've just got to get on with it. Next week would be the Bully Wee, another famous Glasgow side who now play their football in Cumbernauld. And it was to be a Sunday kick-off, 12.45pm – I couldn't wait!

Quote of the day – *Wife: 'Who are they playing today?' 'Queen's Park,' I replied. 'Is that the team that play at mini Hampden?' Yes dear! (Mini does sound better than lesser I suppose).*

GAME	RANGERS VERSUS QUEEN'S PARK
COMPETITION	SFL3
DATE	SATURDAY 20 OCTOBER 2012, 3PM
VENUE	IBROX STADIUM
ATTENDANCE	49,463
SCORE	2-0

Some Views from the Fans

Kenny McKie, age 49, IT Engineer

CLUB *Rangers FC.*

SEASON TICKET *No (did have for 15 years).*

FIRST GAME

Rangers v Airdrie.

BEST MEMORY

Rangers v Fiorentina.

WORST MEMORY

Season 2011/12.

BEST FOOTBALL QUOTE

'I'll shove that microphone up his arse' – Archie Knox about Chic Young.

IS THE BAW BURST?

It's seriously deflated.

How will the situation at Rangers affect Scottish football?
It is obvious that Rangers being in the Third Division has a serious impact on the SPL and its ability to generate money. However, every other club in Scotland benefits from playing Rangers as they climb back through the Divisions. The national team also suffers as a result of the decision not to select Rangers players.

Will the 'new' Rangers differ from the liquidated company or is it business as usual, albeit in a different league?
No, it's business as usual. The only thing that has changed is the parent company name. Rangers are still the same club, despite the efforts of others.

The 'new' Rangers are plying their trade in Division Three. Was this the right decision?
Yes. The situation with the SPL clubs had become untenable. They say they don't want/need Rangers, but certainly want / need the money that Rangers generate for them. Strangely, this was a case when the Turkeys did actually vote for Christmas.

What does the future hold for Rangers and Celtic, assuming Rangers make it back to the top tier of Scottish football?
Sadly, more of the same. Limited success in European competition, by way of qualifying, and a resumption of the age old hostilities, only this time with more vitriol due to the campaign to sink Rangers that was plainly orchestrated by those with a different and sinister agenda. Paranoid? No, just not blind.

What do we need to do to improve Scottish football?
- Restructuring of the leagues.
- Salary cap.
- Maximum squad sizes.
- One governing body instead of three.
- A clear-out at the top of Scottish football, bringing in experienced business people who won't be blinded or influenced.

James Robinson, age 31, area sales manager

CLUB   *Cowdenbeath.*

SEASON TICKET   *No.*

FIRST GAME

Now you're asking, so long ago!

BEST MEMORY

Promotion to the First Division.

WORST MEMORY

Finishing with the lowest points and goal difference when relegated from First Division.

BEST FOOTBALL QUOTE

'He who plays for himself plays for the opposition.'

IS THE BAW BURST?

Naw, it just needs pumped up.

How will the situation at Rangers affect Cowdenbeath Football Club?
It won't affect us directly (well unless you include our chairman Donald Findlay), but depending on how our season and Rangers' season goes we may meet in the Second Division next season. Which I think would be a good thing as the revenue would be much needed.

How will the situation at Rangers affect Scottish football?
I think it may well be a good thing as it will bring in much needed revenue for the smaller clubs who Rangers play. It will also help Rangers bring young players through the ranks instead of going out and buying players. This in turn will help the standard of future Scottish players coming through the ranks.

As an example, I did some work for a guy who is friends with someone involved with Arbroath FC, when Rangers played them at Arbroath's ground in the cup they took enough money to keep the club going for two seasons. This can only benefit the smaller clubs.

Cowdenbeath have played in the top tier of Scottish football, how do they get back to that level?
New stadium, new investment in the club and playing squad.

The Blue Brazil has some of the most fervent fans in the game, how do we get more of them through the gates on a Saturday?
That's a difficult question, I think if the football on show was of a higher standard you may well see the gates improve. I also think deals should be done to get school kids through the turnstiles, this in turn would hopefully help with them supporting a local team. More needs to be done with the club and the community, which I think is beginning to happen.

What do we need to do to improve Scottish football?
The Scottish game is going through a difficult time at the moment, I feel more investment is needed in grass-roots football, more all-weather pitches would help and better coaching for kids which would help bring the standard up. Trying to get some allocated time on all-weather pitches is almost impossible and is very expensive. Maybe the SFA and Scottish Government can assist with the costs to help get people active.

14

CLYDE V RANGERS

Another Glasgow Derby

HOT ON THE HEELS of the first 'Original Glasgow Derby' in over 50 years, Rangers travelled to Cumbernauld to face another team that originated in the south side of the city. Clyde were the hosts for the early Sunday kick-off. Big dilemma! The English Premiership was looking very tasty again this afternoon. First up was the Merseyside clash between Everton and Liverpool and then Chelsea versus Manchester United. Very appealing indeed. But I had secured my ticket for Broadwood midweek and, after missing out on the Stirling Albion game and the recent internationals in Wales and Cardiff, it was SFL3 for me.

I headed north through the wind and torrential rain. The clocks went back the previous night and winter was here already – definitely my least favourite weekend of the year. This fixture was the type that many had predicted would see Rangers struggle. A typical 'sleeves rolled up' encounter in cold, wet conditions. Would the 'full-time, big-money' boys handle the 'in-your-face part-timers' who were playing in their first 'cup final' of the season. Add to the mix, a dodgy pitch (that would only get worse during the game) and Rangers woeful away form and suddenly the big price for the home side looked tempting! That all changed en route to the game.

One of my recommendations from *Is The Baw Burst?* was that 'smaller' clubs should consider a plastic surface. Annan and Forfar, for example, have gone down this route and will reap the benefits. Radio Scotland reported that Clyde have also just installed the 4G but as they don't own their stadium the financial aspect will not be as rewarding. But from a footballing perspective it should make a significant difference – a good playing surface is conducive to good football.

It can be used all year round and more importantly encourages the passing game. The Radio Scotland commentary team was discussing the merits of artificial surfaces while I sat stationary on the slip road from the M80. The pundits (including former players) all agreed that the preference would always be grass and I concur. However, grass needs to be in good condition and maintained to a very high standard – that costs money. Yes, we would all love an Emirates quality pitch but that's not realistic for most Scottish clubs and the sooner we get more of these artificial pitches laid in this country the better.

Twenty minutes after leaving the motorway, I was parked at St Maurice's High School. I had expected to be in the supporters' car park adjacent to the ground as per my last visit. The Wee Rangers were the visitors that day and 771 supporters watched the English side run out easy winners. Little planning was required for those Third Division encounters two years ago – things were slightly different this time around. The school was only ten minutes walk from the ground and I was soon looking for a programme seller. Enquiries confirmed that they were on sale inside the ground. I headed for the west stand (closed the last time I was here) passing numerous supporters selling tickets (where were they getting them from?) and after a short queue, I squeezed through the turnstile. No time for food or drink. No sign of any programmes either, for the second week in a row! Game on at Broadwood.

The teams lined up and dutifully adhered to the anti-racism campaign protocol. Many fans (lots in fancy dress) were still making their way to their seats when the ref started the game. It was great to see the wee place almost full. What a boost the Third Division has had from Rangers this season – extended leagues are definitely the way forward. But the visitors were in no mood for benevolence on the pitch. They started well and dominated the early stages. The passing was fast and slick on the new surface. It looked great to play on and I'm sure the constant drizzling rain was making it even faster.

With 17 minutes gone, Dean Shiels curled a lovely shot into the top corner of the net. Rangers had the lead and were playing well. In fact, it was easily the best away performance I had witnessed this season. Would today be the day when we battered a few goals in? I'd spoken too soon. Ordinary is the only way to describe the rest of the half. The Bully Wee should have equalised after a good move, but it wasn't to be and the visitors headed up the tunnel 1-0 up.

I headed for the pie stall and took my place in a lengthy queue. It

Lesser Shawfield: Home of Clyde but for how much longer?

moved quickly and I was soon at the counter. Pie (mince – no steak left) and Bovril cost me £4. The pie was only lukewarm (yuck) and I again thought about the arrangements in the smaller grounds. Broadwood is a modern stadium and should have adequate facilities for the 7,500 people it can seat. Yet this council-run venue was lacking in the catering department. Yes, it was far better than Berwick or Forres in this respect but overall I think there is room for improvement. More planning is required for Rangers' next visit.

The second half continued along the same lines as the first. Rangers failed to get a grip on proceedings, and frustrations were mounting on and off the park. Ian Black remonstrated with his own supporters after they criticised his poor corner kick. Tackles were meaty and elbows were flying. The expected one-way traffic towards the home side's goal never materialised. Alexander tipped an excellent Clyde effort over the bar. The Gers were struggling away from home again – the next goal would be very important. Then a handbag war broke out. Clyde's Neill threw his at Rangers' Shiels. A few others got involved before the referee intervened and dismissed the Bully Wee midfielder. With the home side down to ten men, the outcome was inevitable.

Rangers, somewhat unconvincingly, sealed the points when top scorer McCulloch prodded home from close range after 80 minutes. Unfortunately for the home side, it was game over. They had performed well though, and should take a lot of credit from the match. The goal had signalled a mass exodus from the stadium but I waited to the end to applaud the first away win in the league this season – it was nearly November!

I was soon on the M80 and motoring home. Radio 5 Live was building up the Chelsea v Manchester United match and I decided to go straight home and watch it rather than go to the gym! Two years ago, I was watching Rangers hold the Red Devils to a draw at Old Trafford. It really is incredible how far the club has fallen. Instead of a Champions League match to look forward to midweek, it was Inverness Caledonian Thistle at Ibrox in the League Cup. The next Saturday, it would be Alloa in the Scottish Cup. Ally McCoist stated during that week that he was envious of Celtic's trip to the Nou Camp for their tie against Barcelona. I was too. But it will be a long time before Rangers are back in Europe's elite club competition.

Celtic's performance in Spain was widely acclaimed and rightly so. They defended superbly. But so did the Gers when they played United in Manchester (parked the bus game) and Barcelona at home (anti-football comment from Messi) and away ('Papac was defending in Malaga' comment from McCoist) yet the post match analysis was generally negative. Why the difference? You play to your strengths to get a result. Every Third Division team this year has done just that, and made things hard for the Glasgow giants. No complaints from the club or fans – just get on with it.

That was the first quarter of an intriguing season over. As expected, Rangers topped the table but it had been a difficult ride so far, particularly away from home in the strange wee stadiums. But in that respect, it had been refreshingly different. Many of the fans (and players) would never have been to some of the grounds so it was a welcome change from the constant drudgery of the SPL.

The smaller clubs are benefiting enormously from the Ibrox club playing in the fourth tier – some have been completely revitalised. The fans have gotten behind Rangers in their thousands. Attendance records have been broken throughout the division. Old rivalries re-ignited. I think it's been enlightening. Personally, I've not missed the Old Firm games at all. We definitely needed a break from all of that nonsense. One thing that doesn't change is the expectation levels of the Rangers. Whether it's Celtic or Clyde, Berwick or Barcelona, the Gers must win!

Quote of the day – *Rangers fan: 'Brilliant Perry, pish Perry.' The big Rangers defender went on a mazy run that lasted less than a second!*

GAME CLYDE VERSUS RANGERS

COMPETITION SFL3

DATE SUNDAY 28 OCTOBER 2012, 12.45PM

VENUE BROADWOOD

ATTENDANCE 7,500

SCORE 2-0

Some Views from the Fans

Colin McCabe, age 30, civil engineer

CLUB   *Rangers.*

SEASON TICKET   *Yes.*

FIRST GAME

Rangers v Morton (1987).

BEST MEMORY

Being at Tannadice the night Rangers won nine in a row.

WORST MEMORY

Losing out on ten in a row, the manner of losing the UEFA Cup final, liquidation.

BEST FOOTBALL QUOTE

'Let the others come after us. We welcome the chase.'

IS THE BAW BURST?

Yes.

How will the situation at Rangers affect Scottish football?
At this stage it looks like the Rangers situation in isolation won't affect Scottish football. However, the combined effect of other problems within Scottish football will push at least one other club down the same road as Rangers. The trouble being for smaller clubs – they don't have the fan base or external appeal that Rangers command. If another Premier League team goes to the wall (other than Celtic) I would be surprised if they were to make a recovery. For instance, if Kilmarnock were to go to the wall – would they have the ability to make it back in any shape or form?

For teams outwith the Premier League it is only going to have a positive influence on their finances as Rangers pass through the leagues.

Will the 'new' Rangers differ from the liquidated company or is it business as usual, albeit in a different league?
Having been to home and away games this season, there doesn't feel to be any difference around the club. Home games, it's the same as last year, at the away games there doesn't feel any difference except the locations. The

feeling about the club is no different – I would say that the feeling during administration was worse. There was an air of collapse of an empire last year, whereas this year there is more positivity within the supporters, a real will to stick by the club and be there to see them back to the top.

As far as the running of the business is concerned I think Green is a shrewd individual. It is a little disconcerting that there have been no redundancies, no obvious cuts except the players that left, from a business that was losing £10million a year last year. It would be good if Green were to come out and spell out how the business is operating.

I'm not sure of the wisdom of things carrying on as normal, will it do the players any good? Is this the reason the players aren't performing away from home? Should a team playing in the Third Division be treating their players like Premier League stars?

The 'new' Rangers are plying their trade in Division Three. Was this the right decision?
I think it was the correct decision for Rangers to play in the Third Division. Once liquidation was an inevitability and a newco had to be formed there was no other option. The other Premier League teams were put in an impossible position by their 'so-called' supporters. I genuinely believe all the talk of sporting integrity and clubs being boycotted if Rangers got back in to be total nonsense and a front for underlying hatred built up over the last 30 years of Rangers dominance and (say it quietly) arrogance. If the bulk of this opinion came from Celtic supporters I could understand it. Celtic got their house in order over the last 15 years or so while Rangers were racking up massive debts and winning leagues etc. However, Celtic fans still fill their ground every other week, where as Dundee Utd, Aberdeen, St Mirren, etc can't muster a sell-out – even when the Old Firm fill three sides of their grounds. Rangers and Celtic have bank-rolled these teams for far too long and at the one moment when Rangers needed one hand up they got kicked in the teeth.

What does the future hold for Rangers and Celtic, assuming Rangers make it back to the top tier of Scottish football?
I think it will be business as usual when Rangers get back to the Premier League. Albeit, Rangers will find in front of them a much stronger Celtic both financially and the team on the pitch.

What do we need to do to improve Scottish football?
There needs to be a complete root and branch shake down. The SPL, SFL and SFA should amalgamate. I'm interested to see if the influence of

performance chief Mark Wotte will start to make a difference in the next few years. Education is a massive part of creating dedicated footballers. How often have we heard of players with potential falling away after they break into the first teams of our bigger clubs. Money and fame seem to ruin most young players in Scotland... and how many times have we heard of players we maybe know locally or grew up with that once they found 'women and drink' their football career is cast adrift?

At the moment, Scotland are the poor cousins within European football, we need to be more creative. We don't have the same TV money as English clubs so we must create our own players and play and trade our way out of lack of funds. The joke of the situation is that the bulk of the cash that English clubs get from TV companies is squandered on overrated, overpaid, often average players.

Other comments

If all stakeholders within Scottish football – clubs, fans and authorities – go about their business in the correct fashion the Rangers situation will be the catalyst for a renaissance within the game in Scotland. However, in true Scottish footballing fashion, we will no doubt shoot ourselves in the foot and make an even bigger mess of the situation than we are already in.

George Wilson, age 82, health and safety consultant

CLUB   *Clyde FC.*

SEASON TICKET   *Yes. An Executive ticket.*

FIRST GAME

1939 Scottish Cup Final.

BEST MEMORY

Winning the Scottish Cup in the 1950s when we had a team boasting five international players including Murphy (Ireland), Haddock, Robertson, Ring and Baird (Scotland).

WORST MEMORY

Going into administration circa 2009.

BEST FOOTBALL QUOTE

Matha Gemmell, the famous Clyde trainer who, when asked to be Queen's Park trainer, said he would accept 'if I can get away every Saturday to see the Clyde'.

IS THE BAW BURST?

No, Clyde are not only surviving, but now living within their means.

How will the situation at Rangers affect Clyde Football Club?

It's sad it happened. However it should lead to all clubs realising how important it is to live within their means. Clyde are currently doing this and are hoping to clear off all their debt in the not so distant future.

Rangers in the Third Division will boost the income of all lower division clubs and I'm sure they will enjoy coming to Broadwood as our facilities are great, especially in comparison to some of the other Third Division grounds which are very basic.

Note: My grandfather attended the Clyde's first game at Barrowfield Park in 1877. Then my father. The first game I attended was the 1939 cup final.

How will the situation at Rangers affect Scottish football?

I would suggest it will make all clubs realise they must live within their means, as many of the lower division clubs have always tried to do. It's a shame for Rangers' supporters, but it may demonstrate that all clubs must live within their income and not depend upon 'so called' benefactors buying them out.

Rangers can arise as a better club than they were, with an appreciation of the great work done by directors of clubs in the lower divisions of football who are not given the credit they deserve

The Bully Wee will play Rangers at Broadwood shortly and at Ibrox in the coming months. In what ways will these matches differ from 'normal' Third Division fixtures?

It will give the Clyde's young team a taste of what may be ahead for them if they buckle down and train hard. Rangers will have an advantage playing at Broadwood because the park and dressing rooms are as good as those in the Premier Division unlike other Third Division parks where players can feel the breath of supporters who could reach over and touch them. This can intimidate young Rangers players and may be the reason their away results are so bad.

What does the future hold for Clyde, bearing in mind that the club have slid down the divisions in recent seasons and now seem to be rooted at the lower end of senior Scottish football?

At present, Clyde are looking to leave Broadwood and are looking for a new park back near the Shawfield Area. They are well on their way to becoming financially sound again, and will rise from the ashes to bring back happier days.

Perhaps I will not live to see it. However I have the utmost faith that the good people, who are my friends, on the Clyde board will achieve their objectives.

What do we need to do to improve Scottish football?

A return to when the home club took their match expenses for the match income, which was then divided between the two teams. After all it takes two teams to make it a game of football.

Other comments

'When the one great scorer comes to write against your name [a person or a football club] / He'll write not that you won or lost but how you played the Game. *Grantland Rice*

Jackie Wales, age 46, biomedical scientist

CLUB *Celtic.*

SEASON TICKET *No.*

FIRST GAME

Celtic v Rosenburg.

BEST MEMORY

Celtic v Porto UEFA final, 2003.

WORST MEMORY

Getting beat by Rangers on last day of season.

BEST FOOTBALL QUOTE

'Game of two halves.'

IS THE BAW BURST?

No.

How will the situation at Rangers affect Celtic Football Club?
I don't believe it will, Celtic are a big club, if they can beat Barcelona, they can do anything.

How will the situation at Rangers affect Scottish football?
I think at first the worry was it would be the beginning of the end but it's allowing the Hibs, Motherwell, Dundee Utd to compete for the title and European football.

The 'new' Rangers are plying their trade in Division Three. Was this the right decision?
Not sure, for SPL absolutely, why should they get away with what Livingston and some Italian teams didn't get away with? They broke the rules, they pay the price.

What does the future hold for Celtic and Rangers, assuming Rangers make it back to the top tier of Scottish football?
Rangers don't exist and if they continue to trade as Rangers and they want to keep their history, part of that history is a big tax bill which they should be made to pay. I think by the time Rangers make it back to the SPL Celtic may have joined a different league, perhaps one of the European leagues or one the English leagues.

What do we need to do to improve Scottish football?
Home grown players, encourage more young people into the game.

15

RANGERS V INVERNESS CALEDONIAN THISTLE

The End!

THE PROCESS STARTED on St Valentines day and ended on Hallowe'en. A judge in a courtroom somewhere officially liquidated the 'oldco' Rangers on 31 October 2012. Technically, 140 years of blood, sweat, tears and joy were history. Well, maybe that would be the case for the majority of businesses, but not for a football club and certainly not for Rangers Football Club. We are alive and kicking! To be honest, I wasn't even aware that things were going on behind the scenes. The club, according to chairman Malcolm Murray's programme notes, was going from strength to strength. 'In my 30 years of stock market experience I have never seen a company turnaround from near extinction to where we are now', he said. From a business point of view, things had stabilised. The club was on a firm financial footing and future prospects looked promising. But what about the team? The new Rangers were about to face SPL opposition for the second time this season. It would undoubtedly be a huge challenge and time to find out if the playing side of things was progressing in a similar manner to the business side.

I dropped into the Swallow Hotel for a quick pint before the match. Now, I'm not superstitious but the last time I was in there was the night that Queen of the South beat us in the Ramsdens Cup – nightmare! Hopefully the lads would put in a performance similar to the one against Motherwell (who were then top of the SPL) in the last round. I expected them to be right up for the game. It was another chance for the players to prove to everyone that they were in fact Premier League calibre rather than Third Division. The pundits on Radio Scotland agreed. They expected a different Rangers. All of the motivational factors required to improve performance levels were obvious in the build up. They were playing for a place in a semi-final, pride, national

I could murder a pint!

recognition and the chance to show the detractors that they made the correct decision to come to or stay with Rangers. I was excited about the match.

A few minutes after leaving the hotel I was in my usual seat, reading through the Hallowe'en edition of Ready. It was much quieter than normal, which was a bit disappointing. I had expected a better turnout for the form team in the SPL. The game kicked off under the floodlights on a perfect night for football. There was plenty of singing and bouncing to get the players going. Typically, the noisy Gers fans were having a go at the SPL. The hatred for the organisation that runs the top tier of Scottish football is alarming. If Rangers ever get back to a position where a return to the SPL is the next step, will the fans – or the club for that matter – want to rejoin? I doubt it. The aversion to everything SPL (and SFA) is deep-rooted and unlikely to diminish in the foreseeable future. Where does that leave Scottish football? I really do fear for the game in this country.

The match started at a good tempo and was entertaining in the opening stages. The two teams looked evenly matched, although in reality Inverness were controlling the game. Rangers, as expected, took the play to the visitors who were content to sit back and comfortably soak up the pressure. This was the case until the 27th minute when the highlanders broke the deadlock. A simple ball in between two Gers defenders was enough for former Murray park starlet Shinnie to slip the ball past Alexander in the Rangers goal. Oh dear! With the natives getting increasingly restless, the home team huffed and puffed right up to half time. The promise of the early stages had disappeared. Quite simply, Rangers were struggling. Again!

During the break, I tried to work out what the manager could do to change things. Not a lot was my conclusion. He could move players into different positions but I don't think that would have made much difference. The bench didn't offer any solutions either. Inverness looked stronger in every department; it really was men against boys and this is one of the main problems that Rangers (and all other clubs) have to contend with. The fans love to see the youngsters coming through the ranks – I'm the same. Indeed, in almost all of the questionnaires returned by fans for this volume of *Is The Baw Burst?* developing young Scottish players is mentioned as the way forward for the game in this country. I fully agree, but they have to be ready for the big time. The Rangers situation is case in point. They have no option but to field young players and, quite simply, they're not up to it. Two years ago I commented on the number of young boys, playing in the lower leagues, who didn't look physically ready. This situation was again staring me in the face.

The second half was all about Inverness. They emphasised their top league status with an assured performance and another two goals. Rangers offered nothing in return. The stadium started emptying long before the final whistle. Over 28,000 had turned up on the night hoping to see their favourites get a victory and a semi-final spot. Some had even fancied a crack at Celtic in the penultimate round or the final. I didn't. We're miles away from that level of football. Ally McCoist agreed, and I admired his honesty. 'I'm extremely aware of how far we've got to travel', said the Rangers manager.

Thankfully, on the way home the radio guys talked about football rather than the nonsense that I was subjected to on the way to the match. At least 15 minutes were wasted talking about Rudi Skacel's new shirt number – utter drivel – get a grip, lads! Terry Butcher and his boys had a fair jaunt back up north but it would be a lively one. The big man was delighted by his team's performance and it was clear during his interview that he still considered beating Rangers to be a major achievement. This was interesting because I thought Inverness were clear favourites. I had hoped we could sneak it though! The old heart still rules the head when it comes to this football club.

So another chance of silverware was gone. The following Saturday, Second Division Alloa would be the visitors in the third round of the Scottish Cup. Incredible – but this had now become a must win game!

Quote of the day – *'Whit's he on the deck fur ref? Has his hairband fell oot?'*

GAME	RANGERS VERSUS INVERNESS CALEDONIAN THISTLE
COMPETITION	SCLC QF
DATE	WEDNESDAY 31 OCTOBER 2012, KO 7.45PM
VENUE	IBROX STADIUM
ATTENDANCE	28,033
SCORE	0-3

Some Views from the Fans

Neil Thomson, age 42, project manager

CLUB   *Aberdeen.*

SEASON TICKET   *No.*

FIRST GAME
St Mirren (A).

BEST MEMORY
Scottish Cup 1990.

WORST MEMORY
League decider v Rangers, 1991.

BEST FOOTBALL QUOTE
'He bursts into the Box. Kuntz!'

IS THE BAW BURST?
Definitely on the soft side!

How will the situation at Rangers affect Aberdeen Football Club?
No great detriment, income only marginally affected. Positives are offered
– greater chance of league success.

How will the situation at Rangers affect Scottish football?
To Scottish football's benefit, opens up competition in the SPL, gives the
SFL teams a new side to hate!

**Motherwell, St Johnstone, Hearts and Dundee United have all been elimi-
nated from Europe in their first round of matches. How can we improve
on this dismal annual statistic?**
Start the league season earlier to give time for match fitness and new
players to gel and get a competitive edge. But if they are beaten by better
teams, not much can be done about that.

What do we need to do to improve Scottish football?
Disband both Old Infirm teams – frees up many thousands of fans from
making weekly trips to Glasgow to instead support their local teams. Also

removes the huge imbalance that they bring to Scottish football.

Other comments
- Gear Scottish football up to supporting the national side as the overriding priority, use the German model.
- Success at international level will reflect well and benefit the club game.
- Stop trying to emulate the English leagues – they are a different scale of operation and are not therefore a fair comparison.
- Look to more similar sized countries instead. Improve facilities, especially training and indoor – get community/local council ownership of grounds etc.

Scott Christie, age 31, senior engineering technician

CLUB *Raith Rovers.*

SEASON TICKET *Yes.*

FIRST GAME

Raith v Ayr, 1987.

BEST MEMORY

Winning League Cup / Bayern Munich games

WORST MEMORY

All derby defeats, 7-1 home loss to Ross County.

IS THE BAW BURST?

Yes.

How will the situation at Rangers affect Raith Rovers Football Club?
It won't have a significant impact on RRFC.

How will the situation at Rangers affect Scottish football?
Some SPL clubs will have a slight drop in revenue, however I don't think this will be as bad as the media and members of the SFA/SPL have described. There will be a boost to the lower leagues as Rangers try and make their way back up the leagues.

Raith Rovers had a very successful period in the nineties. Can that be repeated and what would be required?
The financial gulf between the SPL and SFL is so large that success on that scale is very unlikely.

What do we need to do to improve Scottish football?
Better focus on youth development, however this is difficult if clubs have no money. More artificial surfaces and possibly summer football.

Close the financial gap between the top two divisions and restructure the leagues to larger divisions with an expanded League Cup with group stages to cover any matches lost due to less league games.

The lack of real competition and high ticket prices are the main reasons for poor attendances.

16

RANGERS V ALLOA

A Magnificent Seven

THE FINAL GAME of the first part of this season's journey was upon me. The Scottish Cup tie against Alloa was a massive game for the new Rangers. The comprehensive midweek defeat against Inverness Caledonian Thistle had stunned the supporters. Manager Ally McCoist was under serious pressure. His record in cup competitions as a manager was dreadful, and going out of three cup competitions in as many months would be too hard to swallow. Victory against the Second Division high-flyers was a must. Alloa would be buoyed up after the Rangers cup defeat to Inverness and would fancy their chances. The match would be a real challenge for us but things had to improve.

McCoist wasn't the only manager under pressure that weekend. The SFA had yet to decide if Scotland boss Craig Levein would remain in the hot seat. They made Levein wait for three weeks before they relieved him of his duties on Monday 5 November. If I were in his shoes I would've walked the week before. The board was obviously split on whether he could continue or not and they must have reached a deadlock situation. If he did stay on, he'd need to work with people who clearly didn't think he was the right man for the job. And with the Tartan Army calling for his head, I think his position was untenable.

Personally, I would have given him one more crack at it. I don't think chopping and changing managers is good for the game. But it's not my decision and yet again the SFA hierarchy are looking like an incompetent bunch. Top executives need to make swift decisions. That's why they're in the job, that's what everyone expects and that's why they're on the big money. Gordon Strachan is the fans' and bookies' favourite to be the next national manager – speedy decision making by those two groups. But I wonder how long the SFA will take to appoint somebody?

John Grieg guarding the Big Hoose.

It was good going to the football on a Saturday for a 3pm start. Incredibly, it was only the third time this season that a game had kicked off at the traditional start time at Ibrox – and it was November! This needs to change. I have commented previously on the 3pm start – asking if it is the right time to kick-off on a Saturday. I would prefer 2pm as that suits my lifestyle better. But the important thing is consistency. That's what the fans want. I don't care what the TV channels demand, it shouldn't be about them or their money. It's about time we made a stand on this one. Football should be played at the same time every Saturday, end of story.

On the train up to Glasgow, I was surprised to read that Terry Butcher had been installed as favourite to replace McCoist as manager of Rangers. The big man had incurred the wrath of the Ibrox faithful after Wednesday's match. He was delighted with the result and went over to celebrate with the travelling supporters. Some Gers fans took umbrage to 'one of their own' celebrating a victory against their team. I wondered if he would be the fans' favourite to take over from McCoist. Another surprising statistic was the price for Alloa to beat

Rangers. Fourteen to one must surely be the longest odds ever offered on a side from the Second Division to beat a team playing in the Third Division. I'm sure many people would have had to look twice at that one!

I headed for the Megastore as soon as I arrived at the stadium. I still needed a programme from the Queen's Park match and hoped to pick one up in there. No luck in the store, so I headed into the main stand for some lunch. After the £5 meal deal was polished off, I read through the afternoon's programme. In his notes, McCoist commented on the expectation levels at the club. He is in no doubt that they need to be lowered and I totally agree. It's hard, but we need to remember that we are a Third Division club. We're building a new team and rebuilding the business. It will take time to get to the stage where we can emulate the successes of the past. We'll need to get used to getting beat now and again, particularly when we come up against SPL clubs. Easier said than done!

The game kicked off in front of 25,478 people and within a minute, the majority of them were on their feet. Dean Shiels scored for Rangers and silenced the sizeable Alloa support. Would today be the day when we finally scored the barrow-load we'd been waiting for? It certainly looked that way early on. The home side were right up for it and added another two before half time. The Wasps struggled to get a foothold in the game, which was disappointing. Paul Hartley had them playing good football and I had been looking forward to seeing the reigning Third Division champions perform. But Rangers' early goal knocked the stuffing out of them and they were lucky to go in at half time only three down.

The second half was the same story. Rangers dominated and scored another four goals. My long-awaited goal fest had materialised – what were we saying about expectation levels? The Blue Order sang the praises of Super Ally; he would have been both delighted and relieved. Who knows what would have happened if the result went the other way? The team had responded to the midweek defeat in spectacular fashion. Interestingly, the 11 Rangers players on the park at the end had an average age of just over 23 years. Take Alexander and McCulloch out of that equation and it drops to just over 21 years. This must have been one of the youngest groups ever to play for the first team, and the majority of them were Scottish as well. Hopefully the team will continue to develop along these lines. That's what the fans have been crying out for, pity it took liquidation to get our way.

So seven goals meant seven pints – I had been awarding myself a pint for every home goal. We headed for the Old Toll Bar for a couple before hitting the city centre. It had been a good day.

Quote of the day – *Rangers fans: 'Greek boy's playing well today', 'Aye he must have a twin.'*

GAME	RANGERS VERSUS ALLOA ATHLETIC
COMPETITION	SC R3
DATE	SATURDAY 3 NOVEMBER 2012, KO 3PM
VENUE	IBROX STADIUM
ATTENDANCE	25,478
SCORE	7-0

Some Views from the Fans

Alexander Bird, age 32, active schools coordinator

CLUB *Dunfermline.*

SEASON TICKET *No.*

FIRST GAME

Dunfermline v Rangers.

BEST MEMORY

Above game 2-0 to Pars, League Cup in the 1980s, Smith and Watson against England and Scotland internationalists.

WORST MEMORY

Cup Final 2007, Celtic 1 Pars 0. Late goal, played well, beaten and relegated.

IS THE BAW BURST?

No.

How will the situation at Rangers affect Dunfermline Athletic Football Club?
On the pitch it doesn't affect me as a fan, the Premier League with them was a two horse race with little interest even with the Pars in it last season. First Division is a competitive league with realistically around six teams having a shout for promotion at the outset.

How will the situation at Rangers affect Scottish football?
I know it is against the thoughts of the majority and seen as financially impossible, but if they are not in the league and Celtic are shifted to a more competitive league then all other clubs start competing to win and no longer for third place. It could bring in more support and a better, more competitive product on the pitch.

As things stand with cost too high and no real chance of winning unless you support the big two, the Premier League was dead with or without Rangers in it.

Dunfermline should be a Premier League club, what needs to be done to maintain top league status?
Dunfermline do well on the pitch now with relatively young Scottish

players. Playing attacking football is good to watch but they need to get the community back on their side. The Pars in the Community programme, which gets young kids playing the sport, is currently not up to standard, it could be real asset to the club in getting young players for the future but also young fans and families immediately.

Periodically we see good crowds at East End Park, particularly for Fife derbies, but how do we get more of them through the gates on a 'normal' Saturday?
A competition with a realistic chance to succeed; people will go to a game where something is played for. Given the chance to win the league for all teams over a period of time, people will attend. £15+ to see a game is too steep even for big games; fill the ground for £5 regularly and people will come and support the team.

What do we need to do to improve Scottish football?
Make it competitive again, the majority of fans outwith the big two seldom see a chance to win, they never lose interest in the local team but never get the chance to grab on to success and get to win the cup/league, or enter Europe.

It may be impossible with current structures, but if we could, we should get shot of the big two. It may seem like suicide, but from the supporters perspective it is the only thing which would draw me back to the Premier League as it stands.

David Todd, age 26, housing maintenance officer

CLUB *Raith Rovers.*

SEASON TICKET *Yes.*

FIRST GAME

Raith v Celtic at Starks.

BEST MEMORY

League Cup Final v Celtic.

WORST MEMORY

Every day during the Anelka reign.

BEST FOOTBALL QUOTE

'I spent a lot of money on birds, booze and fast cars. The rest I just squandered' – George Best.

IS THE BAW BURST?

Naw.

How will the situation at Rangers affect Raith Rovers Football Club?
It gives the leagues a realistic chance of reconstruction. If not, it at least should give the club a boost financially with Rangers coming to Starks at some point. I'm glad Raith were so vocal in supporting fans views in Rangers being put into the Third Division.

How will the situation at Rangers affect Scottish football?
Everyone outside the SPL should really do well out of it. The SPL clubs have made their own living off the Old Firm clubs for too long. Everyone should cut their cloth and live off their own revenue streams rather than rely on the opposition fans to supplement their income – East Fife have done it to us for years! Ha Ha.

Raith Rovers had a very successful period in the nineties. Can that be repeated and what would be required?
Yes, I'd say it can, with the right mix of players anything can happen. The trouble is holding onto good players at the end of their contracts. Clubs offer a few quid more and generally they leave. All of the ingredients are there, hopefully in the next few years we'll get there.

What do we need to do to improve Scottish football?
Fan numbers are getting worse across the board. Really, I think a national return of 'kids for a quid' would help. Getting the next generation of supporters involved is a must. At the moment nothing substantial is being done and getting to the game is expensive.

HALF-TIME REPORT

AS I WRAP UP this book, the first half of the season is almost over. The new Rangers have played every team in the Third Division and sit at the top of the pile. The Old Rangers have been cleared of any wrongdoing in respect of the EBTS that brought the taxman to the door in the first place. A First Tier Tax tribunal has ruled that the payments were loans that could be repaid – this counters the challenge by HMRC that they were illegal. It has been reported that HMRC will appeal the verdict. I wonder if this whole sorry episode could have been avoided. One thing is certain – Scottish football will feel the repercussions for years come. Back to the journey, which so far has been eventful to say the least. Rangers have been eliminated from two cups at home, to the Doonhamers and Highland heroes Inverness Caledonian Thistle. Humbled by the Binos in Stirling and held by Annan, Berwick and Peterhead as they try to come to terms with their new surroundings.

The fourth tier of Scottish football is experiencing a season like no other. Packed stadiums, unprecedented media coverage and the chance to play one of the world's most famous football clubs four times in one season. Rangers joining the Third Division has been the making of some clubs, for others it has been a long overdue but welcome renaissance.

To date, the SPL has survived the loss of one half of the Old Firm. Average attendances are similar to those of previous seasons for most of the teams. Celtic has suffered the most from their great rivals' demise. League gates have dropped by 5,000 and now sit at around 45,000. Hearts are also a worry and a new report, from corporate rescue and recovery specialist Begbies Traynor, makes clear that clubs other than Hearts are enduring extremely difficult financial situations that are likely to worsen in the coming months. On a positive note, at the time of writing, Hibernian sit top of the league and Inverness are third. Without Rangers, the SPL has become much more of an open field. Dundee, who took the place of Rangers and started the season as Club 12, are firmly rooted to the bottom of the table.

The road to Rio ended in Brussels for the national team and the manager. Three wins from 12 competitive matches was simply not good enough and the SFA, eventually, relieved Craig Levein of his duties. The focus now shifts to France 2016 for the next European Championships. Our last major tournament, France 1998, seems like a lifetime ago.

The predicted Armageddon for Scottish football has yet to materialise – the rollercoaster roars on but for how much longer? Watch this space.

Let's now review some of the recommendations from the first volume of *Is the Baw Burst?*

A Different League Set-Up?

LEAGUE RECONSTRUCTION

I can guarantee that agreement on the way forward for league reconstruction will happen this season. The fans, and many clubs, are desperate for a shake-up of the four-league system. The new Rangers' venture into the Third Division has been a refreshing change from the endless monotony of the SPL. Yes, there are downsides but one of the many positives is variety and quite simply that has been missing for years. Revisiting all these places with Rangers has been exciting and enlightening – extending the top league will revitalise many clubs and encourage those in the second tier to aim higher.

Charles Green, the Ibrox club's chief executive, has publicly stated that Rangers will never play in the SPL again. The majority of Rangers fans would also be reluctant to engage with anything 'SPL' ever again. I personally don't see a future for the organisation and moves are underway for a radical overhaul. Hearts are currently teetering on the brink of financial catastrophe and others are allegedly in a similar position – Armageddon for the SPL is imminent.

The SFL's proposals for reorganisation mean that the present four tiers would regroup into three leagues of 16, 10 and 18 teams (total 44). This aligns with what many of the fans want but is different to the arrangements favoured by Supporters Direct Scotland. SDS favours two leagues of 16 playing each other twice, with a qualifying league of ten playing each other four times, making up 42 places. In their model, promotion and relegation arrangements are a combination of automatic and play-off places through the three leagues. The SPL claim that this is one way of increasing competition as recommended in Henry McLeish's official review:

> There should be more competition within our professional game. This should be achieved by more promotion and relegation and play-offs between competing leagues. This will provide more interest and more incentive.

There could be two additional teams in the new SFL model. Colt sides from Celtic and Rangers playing in senior football forms part of their proposal to reorganise the Scottish game from season 2015/16 however, resistance from the other 'big clubs' may scupper the Old Firm youth teams. There are differences in both sets of proposals but as McLeish says, the outcome must provide more interest and more incentive. And crucially, it could remove the futile SPL from the equation.

SHOULD THE OLD FIRM DEPART THE SCOTTISH PREMIER LEAGUE?

> It's only when you see the chasing pack that you realise just how big Rangers and Celtic are within the Scottish leagues. They really are in a class of their own and they need a fresh challenge – but where should they go? – *Is the Baw Burst? Volume 1.*

This has never been more apparent. Third Division Rangers remain one of the best-supported clubs in world football. They regularly attract nearly 50,000 people to their home matches. Celtic apart, this dwarfs the combined attendance figures for every other Scottish club on a normal Saturday. The fans see this imbalance as detrimental to Scottish football and I agree. Quite simply, they're too big but they have nowhere to go.

Every week supporters pass by their local stadiums en route to Ibrox and Parkhead. The Old Firm dominate the major prizes and even though Rangers are currently in the bottom tier of the game in this country they can still attract players from clubs in the top division – this is wrong. The challenges for second place in the SPL this season are a good example. Hibernian, Inverness CT and Aberdeen have all upped their game. The Rangers situation has opened up the league and the clubs have responded. If the big two were to depart I think the league would prosper.

The Old Firm dominance argument was perfectly illustrated by last season's Scottish Cup Final – Hearts v Hibs at Hampden on 19 May 2012, a hugely important event for the fans. Hearts legend John Roberston summed it up: 'For one set of fans it will be the greatest day of their lives. For the losers, it will be the toughest of results to take.' For me, the biggest winner was Scottish football because, believe it or not, that was the first time the two clubs have met in the Cup Final since 1896.

The people of Edinburgh, former players of the respective clubs and the fans were all thrilled to be in the final, but why has it taken so long for the Edinburgh clubs to get this chance? I would say that the problem, certainly over the last 12 years, has been down to the Old Firm dominating proceedings, although the two Glasgow giants can't really be held responsible for the limited success of their Edinburgh neighbours in this competition. However, it's clear to me that if Hearts and Hibs were regularly competing to win the league, then they would have more chance of success in this tournament as well.

FRIDAY NIGHT FOOTBALL

I've said previously that I'm in favour of Friday night football. However, my only recent experience to date was the Wales v Scotland international in Cardiff. I watched this one on TV and enjoyed it but it does take a bit of getting used to. I've completely missed many of the SPL Friday night fixtures this season – only realising the next morning when I'm checking the fixtures for the football coupon!

The Scottish Football Season

CHANGE TO A MARCH TO NOVEMBER SEASON

The idea of changing the football season calendar is gathering support. For example, SFA President Campbell Ogilvie recently told the BBC:

> From somebody who always said football must be played from August through to May, I am starting to take a different view of the matter.

Scottish women's and girls' football already has a March to November calendar, and Sheila Begbie, SFA Women's Football Co-ordinator, is convinced of the benefits. She says:

> The rise of the Scotland women's national team and the success of Glasgow City in reaching the last 16 of the Champions League were made possible by the change, with players getting the chance to play more often in weather and surfaces conducive to good football.

Hopefully Marvember will be at the top of the agenda when everyone sits down to discuss league reconstruction. Many of the fans who responded to the *Is the Baw Burst?* questionnaires are also in favour of changing when we play in this country. The main reasons are:

✓ a better chance of getting through the qualifying rounds of the European competitions
✓ better quality football
✓ a better spectator experience

I fully agree with all of the above, they are legitimate reasons for change. Another one is the televised English Premier League (EPL). Spectating in bad winter weather is hard enough. But throw in the carrot of a live EPL game and it's almost too good to resist. On two occasions already this season I've been tempted by top of the table and derby matches in the EPL instead of heading to Ibrox. So far I've resisted, but that could change on a cold, wet January day. In a sense, we are competing with the EPL, which is ludicrous. The top league south of the border is the biggest money-spinner in the world and attracts global sponsorship and advertising. If we scheduled our matches for March through to November there would be fewer fixture clashes and hopefully this would get some armchair fans back to the games in Scotland.

Liverpool manager Brendan Rodgers said recently that his club couldn't compete on all fronts with the big boys. What chance do we have in Scotland if one of England's biggest and most successful clubs is struggling?

Another interesting point is the willingness of Rangers fans to travel in numbers to the Third Division away fixtures so far this season. But with winter fast approaching, the thought of standing on a cold, uncovered terrace in Berwick or Peterhead is just not appealing. I wonder if the fervent support will fade when the weather is at its worst? And another thing – the clubs that still play on grass will experience a significant deterioration of their playing surfaces over the coming months. This affects the quality of the football and the overall spectator experience.

We need to move the season ASAP!

Improving the Stadium Experience

MULTI-USE OF FOOTBALL STADIUMS

Stadiums are a key part of the football infrastructure and should be to a good standard. Scottish stadiums, however, are a real mixed bag with some excellent new modern facilities and some crumbling embarrassments. They need to play a bigger part in the clubs and communities as a whole – even some of the modern ones.

The lack of investment has been going on for years and can't be put down to the recent financial crisis. Not only does it show a real lack of respect for the supporters, it's hardly a good advert for the clubs in terms of attracting fans and players.

This season's travels following Rangers around the Third Division grounds in the country have highlighted lots of shortcomings. Many of the stadiums simply don't have the facilities to cater for any more than a few hundred spectators. Portable toilets and mobile fast food outlets are not acceptable. We need to raise the standards when it comes to stadiums and I don't mean just installing a few seats. Matches that I attended in Berwick, Forres and Peterhead were bearable. Underfoot conditions in Northumberland and Moray were OK because it was dry. On another day they would have been treacherous. Balmoor had a temporary scaffold in place which was better than grass but a section gave way during a 'bounce'! Stadium issues need to be addressed during league reconstruction talks. They are key to going forward.

As I've said before, why would anyone want to spend an afternoon in a dilapidated stadium with poor facilities? Why would children and teenagers want to put up with an environment like that when they could enjoy some time in a virtual world online? Many of the clubs out there have failed the fans in this respect and some could pay the ultimate price – closure – for not being prepared to invest and maintain their infrastructure.

ALL-WEATHER SURFACES

Another important part of the stadium infrastructure is the pitch. Fans and clubs up and down the country are beginning to appreciate the benefits of third and fourth generation artificial surfaces. Annan and Clyde have recently laid new pitches. Berwick want one – Forfar take bookings for their all-weather surface via the local council website. This is definitely the way forward. A revenue stream at the heart of the communities – I guarantee more will follow.

REINTRODUCTION OF TERRACING FOR MATCHES AT ALL LEVELS

I said previously that terracing works without any problems in the lower leagues and we all stand at Hampden for Scotland games – so what are we waiting for? While I fully understand the move to all-seated stadiums after the disasters at Ibrox and Hillsborough, I am firmly of the belief that we should be able to manage safe standing areas in football grounds.

During this latest review I've stood at Peterhead, Berwick, Forres and Hampden twice. It's been OK but, as I said earlier, could have been much worse. Hampden is fine because it's a concrete surface underfoot. As for the rest, they left a lot to be desired and if we are going to go back down this route then the terraced areas need to be of a hard-standing construction. Grassy slopes are not suitable even with a limited number of people on them.

FOOD AND DRINK

Nothing has changed in this respect. At Ibrox, food prices have fallen slightly but the same limited menus remain. Elsewhere it's been a similar story with my lukewarm pie at Broadwood the low point to date. Burger vans still dominate the catering scene and this national problem needs to be addressed. And if you want a pint at a match you'll need to go and watch rugby!

Adding Up the Costs

REDUCED ADMISSION PRICES

What a difference a few divisions makes. Following Rangers is now so much more affordable than before. Ticket prices have plummeted because they are playing in the bottom tier of Scottish professional football and it's been brilliant! My most expensive (Rangers) ticket to date has been £16.80 and that included the infuriating booking fee! The two internationals at Hampden were £25 each and my seat in the Moffat Stand at Rugby Park for the opening day game in the SPL was £17. Home games at Ibrox will cost on average about £15 freeing up roughly £10 for other incidentals.

Fans up and down the country are crying out for cheaper tickets but it's a hard one for the clubs. I'm sure more clubs would like to reduce prices for the fans but would they get the additional numbers through the gates to make up for the shortfall in admission prices? Again the Rangers situation is a good example. Families can again afford to go to a big football match. I paid £38 for two adults and two children for the East Fife League Cup tie – great value and long may it continue.

More Lassies Required

TIME TO ENTICE MORE WOMEN INTO THE GAME

Women are, arguably, football's greatest untapped resource. Has the time come to give them more influence in what can sometimes seem like the last bastion of the male – the beautiful game? Growing numbers of women attend games, but the aim should be to draw more in right across the board.

I must admit I failed when it came to getting more women involved in the debate but that only highlights the imbalance. Family members, friends and colleagues were contacted in my quest to get answers for *Is the Baw Burst?* Volume 2. The questionnaires were issued with suggestions to 'get your friends involved' as well. Unfortunately, only a couple of responses were forthcoming from females. Personally, I don't know of any women that go to the football on a regular basis or are involved. Again, the Rangers saga highlights another problem in football – male dominance. Throughout the administration, liquidation and subsequent rebirth of Rangers, I can't recall any involvement from the fairer sex. The governing bodies are also full of domineering males, many of whom are incompetent, and this needs to change. The London 2012 Olympics and the Scottish women's 'A' team qualification play-off against Spain further highlighted the growing appeal and stature of women's football. The Olympic football tournament captured the imagination of the public; stadiums were full, the football was entertaining and the media coverage finally matched the public interest. In Scotland the girls were desperately unlucky in their attempt to qualify for the female Euros – glorious failure springs to mind!

On the other hand, my wife would have been appalled at some of the things that go on at a match – Berwick and Forres in particular spring to mind. The behaviour of some of the fans left a lot to be desired but as an archetypal football male my response was sadly just a shake of the head and this is probably the root of the problem. For too long we have stood back with 'that's the way it's always been' mentality. Maybe some fresh female eyes would change things for the better!

Leadership Issues

LEADERSHIP REFORMS

Where do I start? The Rangers crisis is the obvious one but the problems were clearly apparent before the monumental collapse of the Glasgow giants. In *Is the Baw Burst?* I wrote:

> Lack of leadership is a major problem for Scottish football. Year after year our teams crash out of Europe at the early stages. Looking back on seasons 2010/11 and 2011/12 it's the same old story – qualifying round failures, often to teams from so-called 'lesser' leagues and without the European pedigree of our teams.

Season 2012/13 started in the usual embarrassing fashion. In no particular order, St Johnstone, Hearts, Dundee United and Motherwell were eliminated from European competitions at the qualifying stages! Celtic on the other hand, have performed admirably in Europe this season and their victory over Barcelona ranks as one of Scottish football's finest achievements. But a one-off every season isn't good enough. We need to do more on the European and international stages and the leaders need to act. This annual European footballing fiasco has been compounded by the administrators' handling of the Rangers situation and subsequent demotion to the Third

Division. The SFA and the SPL struggled to manage the crisis from the outset and appeared to stumble from one decision to another. In my opinion they missed a perfect opportunity to change the game for good in this country. But instead they let the personal agendas, infighting and ill-advised viewpoints (many from fans themselves) obscure the bigger picture and changed course many times. The SFL were left to sort it all out and are due enormous credit for demonstrating the leadership qualities that are so obviously lacking in the other two organisations.

The SFA were also culpable in their handling of the dismissal of the Scotland manager Craig Levein. Their inability to come to a decision left a lot to be desired. Levein was inexcusably made to wait over the weekend for a decision before being relieved of his duties on the Monday. The media, the Tartan Army and almost everybody else knew the manager's time was up so why take so long to come to a decision? Again positive leadership was lacking and it does little to inspire confidence amongst the stakeholders in Scottish football.

So is the Baw Burst?

This is the perennial question. At the outset of the season, I was as positive as I have been for a while on the state of Scottish football. Rangers had survived, the road to Rio was about to begin and fans up and down the country were getting behind their teams. But that has changed significantly in the first few months of the season. The World Cup qualifying campaign ended in Brussels. The fans gallant attempts at selling out stadiums ('Sell Out Saturdays') have fallen by the wayside and Hearts are facing a financial crisis similar to that of Rangers. The Ibrox club appear to be slowly rebuilding and their influence on the Third Division has been significant. The lower tier of Scottish football has had a much-needed boost and is thriving with the Glasgow giants in that league. How the rest of the season will pan out is anybody's guess. But one thing is for sure, there will be plenty of ups and downs still to come – it really is a funny old game!

GET THE DEBATE GOING ON THE BLOG, AT TWITTER OR ON FACEBOOK
HTTP://ISTHEBAWBURST.CO.UK

Also published by Luath Press

Is the Baw Burst? A Long Suffering Supporter's Search for the Soul of Scottish Football

Iain Hyslop

ISBN **978 1 908373 22 9** PBK £9.99

Football has to wake up to reality and get its house in order. Brave decisions must be taken and followed through. Huge changes are needed. Financial problems, falling attendances, poor quality football, crumbling stadiums, terrible catering... is the picture really as bad as it's painted? Time to have a look. IAIN HYSLOP

1 football fan
1 football season
42 football grounds

Written by a football fan, for football fans, this is the unofficial review of the state of Scottish football. Spotting sizable gaps in the review by former First Minister Henry McLeish, Iain Hyslop provides a detailed look at the beautiful game in Scotland.

Every Scottish league ground is visited in a 44 game tour that samples the football, the stadiums, the finances and the pies! Each chapter covers a game from the 2011 season and portrays the experience in a friendly, casual style that resonates with supporters from all over the country. Does Scottish football have a future or is the baw burst?

This view from the not-so-cheap seats (Hyslop is adamant that football has to be more realistic with its pricing policy) ought to be required reading for everyone involved at the top end of the game. THE SCOTSMAN

From Athens to Zagreb: A First-hand History of Hearts in Europe

Mike Buckle

ISBN 978 1908373 41 0 HBK £14.99

From Athens to Zagreb is the complete guide to every game played by Hearts in European competitions since the club became the third Scottish team ever to enter the European Cup.

Here is the essence of the many remarkable games in Hearts' 50-year history in Europe. Benfica, Inter Milan, Atletico Madrid and Bayern Munich – the list of their opponents reads like a who's who of European football. Game by game, the experiences of players, fans and club officials are presented in a montage of frank memories and inimitable pitchside commentary. For Hearts, winning a major European tournament remains an elusive prize, but the faith of the travelling support has been richly rewarded by the many glorious moments chronicled in this book.

With contributions from several prominent Hearts players and celebrity fans, including Ken Stott and Scott Wilson, this book will evoke forgotten memories amongst fans of all ages.

Buckle captures some extraordinary tales in a book guaranteed to stir the sepia-tinted memory banks of anyone who has ever travelled with Hearts.
EDINBURGH EVENING NEWS

Over the Top with the Tartan Army

Andrew McArthur

ISBN 978 0 946487 45 5 PBK £7.99

Thankfully the days of the draft and character-building National Service are no more. In their place, Scotland has witnessed the growth of a new and curious military phenomenon. Grown men bedecked in tartan, yomping across most of the globe, hell-bent on benevolence and ritualistic bevvying. Often chanting a profane mantra about a popular football pundit.

In what noble cause do they serve? Why, football, of course – at least, in theory. Following the ailing fortunes of Scotland isn't easy. But the famous Tartan Army has broken the pain barrier on numerous occasions, emerging as cultural ambassadors for Scotland. Their total dedication to debauchery has spawned stories and legends that could have evaporated in a drunken haze but for the memory of one hardy footsoldier: Andrew McArthur.

Taking us on an erratic world tour, McArthur gives a frighteningly funny insider's eye view of active service with the Tartan Army. Covering campaigns and skirmishes from Euro '92 up to the qualifying drama for France '98 in places such as Moscow, the Faroes, Balarus, Sweden, Monte Carlo, Estonia, Latvia, New York and Finland.

I commend this book to all football supporters... You are left once more feeling slightly proud that these stupid creatures are your own countrymen.
GRAHAM SPIERS

Stramash: Tackling Scotland's Towns and Teams

Daniel Gray

ISBN 978 1906817 66 4 PBK £9.99

Fatigued by bloated big-time football and bored of samey big cities, Daniel Gray went in search of small town Scotland and its teams. Part travelogue, part history, and part mistakenly spilling ketchup on the face of a small child, Stramash takes an uplifting look at the country's nether regions.

Using the excuse of a match to visit places from Dumfries to Dingwall, *Stramash* accomplishes the feats of visiting Dumfries without mentioning Robert Burns, being positive about Cumbernauld and linking Elgin City to Lenin. It is ae fond look at Scotland as you've never seen it before.

... a must-read for every non-Old Firm football fan – and for many Rangers and Celtic supporters too.
DAILY RECORD

There have been previous attempts by authors to explore the off-the-beaten paths of the Scottish football landscape, but Daniel Gray's volume is in another league.
THE SCOTSMAN

A brilliant way to rediscover Scotland.
THE HERALD

I defy anyone to read Stramash *and not fall in love with Scottish football's blessed eccentricities all over again... Funny enough to bring on involuntary, laugh out loud moments.*
THE SCOTTISH FOOTBALL BLOG

Hands on Hearts
Alan Rae with Paul Kiddie
ISBN 978 1 908373 54 0 PBK £9.99

[Rae] was one of the most trustworthy, wonderful, lunatic, crazy, loveable, straight-jacketed men I have ever met in my life. JOHN ROBERTSON (Hearts striker 1981–98; manager 2004–05)

[Rae] was an absolutely fantastic physio who even though he worked in tiny little physio room at Tynecastle got people back from injury very quickly. A wonderful man with a very dry sense of humour who was brilliant company. SCOTT CRABBE (Hearts midfielder/ striker 1986–92)

As Heart of Midlothian FC's physiotherapist, Alan Rae was a vital member of the Tynecastle backroom staff for more than two decades. He was one of the few constants during a tumultuous period in the club's rich history and his behind-the-scenes recollections will fascinate and entertain in equal measure.

From international superstars to mischievous boot-room boys, Rae shares his unique insight into the life of a great Scottish football institution. Hands on Hearts is a must-read for football fans everywhere – Jambos or otherwise – and for anyone who has ever wondered about the healing properties of the physio's magic sponge!

Hands on Hearts *is a rich source of anecdotes about the more unusual characters who were on the club's books during the Rae years.* THE SCOTSMAN

100 Favourite Scottish Football Poems
Edited by Alistair Findlay
ISBN 978 1906307 03 5 PBK £7.99

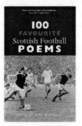

Poems to evoke the roar of the crowd. Poems to evoke the collective groans. Poems to capture the elation. Poems to capture the heartbreak. Poems by fans. Poems by critics. Poems about the highs and lows of Scottish football.

This collection captures the passion Scots feel about football, covering every aspect of the game, from World Cup heartbreak to one-on-ones with the goalie. Feel the thump of the tackle, the thrill of victory and the expectation of supporters.

Become immersed in the emotion and personality of the game as these poems reflect human experience in its sheer diversity of feeling and being.

The collection brings together popular culture with literature, fan with critic, and brings together subject matters as unlikely as the header and philosophy.

[this book] brings home the dramatic and emotional potential that's latent in the beautiful game. THE LIST

Singin I'm No a Billy He's a Tim
Des Dillon

ISBN 978 1 908373 05 2 PBK £6.99

What happens when you lock up a Celtic fan?
What happens when you lock up a Celtic fan with a Rangers fan?
What happens when you lock up a Celtic fan with a Rangers fan on the day of the Old Firm match?

Des Dillon watches the sparks fly as Billy and Tim clash in a rage of sectarianism and deep-seated hatred. When children have been steeped in bigotry since birth, is it possible for them to change their views?

Join Billy and Tim on their journey of discovery. Are you singing their tune?

Explosive. EVENING NEWS

Scotland will never be free of the shackles of sectarianism unless we teach our youngsters that bigotry is wrong. JACK MCCONNELL, MSP, FORMER FIRST MINISTER

His raucous sense of humour and keen understanding of the west-coast sectarian mindset make his sisters-under-the-skin message seem a matter of urgency and not just a liberal platitude. THE GUARDIAN

The sheer vitality of the theatrical writing – the seamless combination of verbal wit and raw kinetic energy, and the pure dynamic strength of the play's structure – makes [Singin I'm No a Billy He's a Tim] feel like one of the shortest and most gripping two-hour shows in current Scottish theatre. THE SCOTSMAN

We Are Hibernian: The Fans' Story
Andy MacVannan

ISBN 978 1906817 99 2 HBK £14.99

We are Hibernian explores the sights, sounds and memories of fans who have taken the 'journey' to watch the team that they love. Supporters from all walks of life bare their souls with humour, emotion and sincerity.

This book celebrates the story behind that unforgettable moment when Hibernian entered the childhood of its fans' lives and why, despite their different backgrounds, these loyal fans still support a sometimes unsupportable cause together.

Is it what happens on the field of play or the binding of tradition, memories and experience that makes Hibs fans follow their team through thick and thin? Featuring interviews with many different fans, this book takes you on a journey to discover why football is more than just a game and why Hibernian is woven into the DNA of each and every one of its supporters.

Everyone walked out that ground like they had just seen the second coming.
Irvine Welsh, writer

My family were Irish immigrants. My father had renounced his Catholicism but had retained a blind faith in Hibs.
Lord Martin O'Neill, politician

In the early 1950s Alan, Dougie and I caught the tail end of the legendary Hibs team when they were still the best team in the world.
Bruce Findlay, music business manager

Luath Press Limited

committed to publishing well written books worth reading

LUATH PRESS takes its name from Robert Burns, whose little collie Luath (*Gael.*, swift or nimble) tripped up Jean Armour at a wedding and gave him the chance to speak to the woman who was to be his wife and the abiding love of his life. Burns called one of the 'Twa Dogs' Luath after Cuchullin's hunting dog in Ossian's *Fingal*. Luath Press was established in 1981 in the heart of Burns country, and is now based a few steps up the road from Burns' first lodgings on Edinburgh's Royal Mile. Luath offers you distinctive writing with a hint of unexpected pleasures.

Most bookshops in the UK, the US, Canada, Australia, New Zealand and parts of Europe, either carry our books in stock or can order them for you. To order direct from us, please send a £sterling cheque, postal order, international money order or your credit card details (number, address of cardholder and expiry date) to us at the address below. Please add post and packing as follows: UK – £1.00 per delivery address; overseas surface mail – £2.50 per delivery address; overseas airmail – £3.50 for the first book to each delivery address, plus £1.00 for each additional book by airmail to the same address. If your order is a gift, we will happily enclose your card or message at no extra charge.

Luath Press Limited
543/2 Castlehill
The Royal Mile
Edinburgh EH1 2ND
Scotland
Telephone: +44 (0)131 225 4326
(24 hours)
Fax: +44 (0)131 225 4324
email: sales@luath. co.uk
Website: www. luath.co.uk